Greetings to the
Kesslers three
Carol, John & William
from their
grandfather Kessler
Easter 1975

FUN FOR THE FAMILY

FUN FOR

THE FAMILY

HARRY D. EDGREN

ABINGDON PRESS
Nashville
New York

*T*his book is dedicated to those families who have found adventure and richness of living in their recreation and to those who may be stimulated to seek the joy of family life and the opportunities for refreshment that come with life through family recreation

Acknowledgments

I am especially indebted to Mrs. "Chris" Brown for writing and illustrating chapter 11; to Mrs. Roger Repp for suggestions and typing the manuscript; to my wife Helen for reading and correcting the manuscript; to Dr. Wellman France for his encouragement and assistance; and to the Recreation Education students of Purdue University, who have been a laboratory for experimentation in activities for family recreation.

Contents

1

FAMILY RECREATION

Why is it important that recreation be a part of family life?
Any discussion today of the functions of the family in the
American way of life includes without question such areas
of concern as democracy, mutual affection, cooperation,
comradeship, social responsibility, and education for the
wise use of leisure. What better place to teach these ideas
than in activities and experiences in the home?

The social influence of the family can come only if there
is sufficient interaction between members of the family.
One of the excellent ways of providing additional occasions
for interaction over and above mealtimes, before bedtime,
etc., is through planned family recreation. The value of
this interaction is that parents can pass on important aspects
of the culture in an enjoyable manner for the child. If the
family provides an interesting environment, there is apt
to be less enticement by undesirable elements of our so-
ciety, and hopefully less parent-child conflict in the period
of adolescence. But children are not the only ones to benefit
from a planned program of family recreation. There is
value for the parents, too, when they have an opportunity
to release excess energy or relax. Aside from these benefits,

11

family recreation of the home variety may be even less expensive than having each member purchase entertainment individually. Family recreation will include activities or interests that meet the needs of each family member, but every member will not necessarily be participating all the time. When recreation is a part of the family, there is more likely to be understanding, sympathy, tolerance, and a general cooperativeness as a part of family life. Leisure then becomes an asset instead of a liability.

Recreation experiences will not be a part of the family life unless someone takes responsibility for bringing them to pass. Some member of the family will need to take the initiative in creating the events in which all the family have experiences which are good and worth continuing in the name of family recreation. Fun becomes a result of sharing and participation in activities which bring satisfaction and happiness to the participant. The needs of affection, recognition, acceptance, and a sense of belonging can be achieved through those activities within the family.

There is no better place to have recreation than the home. Family recreation makes good times inexpensive. It can save us from the tyranny of commercialized and stereotyped recreation. It develops skill among the members of the home in the handling of leisure. It helps to make the house a home.

Many studies show that teen-agers in particular say they have more fun *away* from home, many of them adding that they wished they might have more fun in their homes with their families. It is easy to drift into the pattern of going to the movies, listening to the radio or looking at television, reading comic books and comic papers, and watching athletic events. There is nothing wrong with these activities, but because they are the easiest to do, many people just do them and do not add the important aspect of doing and creating as well as just watching. A balanced family life includes some of each. Parents need to help their children choose and enjoy a variety of recreation.

How does your family rate in this area of family fun? The following set of criteria for measuring the effectiveness of home and family in achieving good family recreation can be used to check your family.

The Home

1. Is space provided where the members of a family can engage in family recreation?

2. Are facilities accessible and in a definite place?

3. Are facilities and equipment kept in good repair?

4. Is it possible to rearrange furniture, remove rugs, etc., in order to provide extra space for recreation?

5. Are new games, crafts, and books purchased occasionally to replenish existing facilities?

6. Are activities and events adapted to various ages of family members?

The Family

1. Is there a willingness on the part of all members of the family to plan creatively for events and special occasions?

13

2. Does the family have an adventurous, exploratory spirit?

3. Has everyone been encouraged to participate in activities alone as well as in groups?

4. Is there an exposure to a variety of recreational activities—physical, social, crafts, music, and dramatics?

5. Have family members been given the chance to increase their skills in various activities?

6. Can everyone swim?

7. Do members make decisions and accept the responsibilities that accompany each decision?

8. Are members associated with causes that are greater than themselves, such as the church, civic and political organizations?

This list might well form the basis for a family discussion on what you as a family can do for fun. It can be the basis for a critical look at what you are now doing, the many things that you might do and are not doing, and can bring about a decision to discuss together and to plan for some activities within the family.

There are several areas of living together where one can set the stage for good family recreation. First of these is the permanent recreational equipment that can be bought or made and which can be used in parlor, basement, or backyard. A good family slogan might be "Buy a good family game for Christmas," thereby contributing a game each year to the family kit or game box. These games become a common means of expression for all members of the family.

Another possibility is table activities following the evening meal. Oftentimes just sitting and listening to a favorite radio or television program makes a later conversation involving the entire family.

Family hobbies are another area in which families can share a common interest. The collecting of maps, photography, playing musical instruments, can become an interest for the entire family as well as for a single person.

Family trips can become gala events instead of just another ride. Weeks before, let the family divide its responsibilities, talk about the route to be taken, and what it will do en route before the destination has been reached. Let these decisions on how to go and what to take along be a family enterprise instead of letting father decide it all.

When visitors come, does the entire family enjoy the visit? Are son and daughter drawn into the conversation, thereby making a family event out of a visit from dad's friends, rather than an occasion when children are annoyed by limitations placed upon them because visitors arrive?

The unusual and different often add greatly to family play. How fortunate is the family which can turn an unexpected or unpredicted event, yes, even a very inconvenient or annoying event, into one of adventure. Try taking the family out on a rainy night in spring or summer, permitting the children to go with heads uncovered allowing the rain to run through their hair. Walk barefoot letting the mud squish up through your toes if you live near the country. The family conversation following such an event becomes one of fun and congeniality.

A family had planned a winter cookout in the woods

near their house. Even though the day became the coldest day of the winter, with the temperature well below zero, they went ahead with their outing (well bundled up, of course). This cookout became one of the family's most cherished memories, on which they often looked back with great pleasure.

When recreation is a part of the family life, the family is playing its vital role along with the church and the school and other private agencies to make life more full and abundant for its members. When parents see this value in family recreation, they will take the initiative and provide for it.

Basic Rules for Family Recreation

1. *Every member shares in planning.* Each member of the family has his say on what is to be done, and an effort is made to work his idea into the program.

2. *Every member has a part in the doing,* both of the work and of the fun.

3. *Fun is worth the doing, even if done poorly.* Forget that copybook maxim, "Be the labor great or small, do it well or not at all." Wherever that maxim may apply, it does *not* apply to family recreation.

4. *Start where you are.* Family recreation begins with existing interests of its members and moves on to new interests. Exploring for new things to do can be fun in itself: looking up what to see on trips, searching out new games, investigating handicrafts and other possible hobbies.

16

2

EQUIPMENT AND GAMES

Equipment is a necessary part of most activities. Having equipment around the home is a stimulation for individuals to start a particular activity. For children, this may be a swing—a long rope supported from a strong tree. For older children, this could be a croquet set, a badminton set, or a table tennis set. For adults, this could be the equipment for boccie ball or a quoits layout.

Equipment like the above should be both available and in easy access for all members of the family—perhaps on a shelf, in a drawer, or in a closet to which members of the family can go, knowing that that is where they can find all recreation equipment.

Families who believe in gathering material for family fun could make it a practice to purchase each year at Christmastime a family game of substantial nature that will last for years to come: a bowling game, a game like Carroms, indoor horseshoes, rubber quoits, or table tennis.

Hobby Room

Where space will permit, a separate game or hobby room can be a real asset in the development of a family

17

recreation program. It serves not only as a spot where the members of the family can play in their leisure time, but also as a gathering place for friends of each member of the family and for joint family events.

In order to consider all these possibilities, the following items are noted as suggested facilities and equipment that will add to the expanded use of a hobby room. For more active use, such games as short-court shuffleboard, with the layout of the court also being used for hopscotch, should be considered. When table tennis is to be added, it is advisable to have a folding table so it can be removed to make space available for other activities. Dart boards, archery, baseball, and other sport targets are other possible additions of interest to all ages. To avoid the danger of injury, it is advisable to use rubber suction or magnetic darts instead of the steel-tip points.

Other facilities such as movie and slide projectors, screen, and a record player will add greatly to the use of this room. A dark room for the developing and printing of pictures will be a stimulation to encourage the family to take up photography as a hobby.

Although very fine games and equipment can be purchased in the store, it is my belief that games made by members of the family have a greater value to the family, both in the making as well as in the use thereafter. Homemade games can be made from the odds and ends found around the home. Use bottle caps or golf tees for checkers. Linoleum blocks, rubber heels or jar rubbers make excellent markers for tossing games. Empty plastic detergent bottles make good tenpins.

Uses of Homemade Game Equipment

1. A game creation night. Have materials available and have family and other friends make games for this one evening. This is in itself a good social activity.

2. Use these games as a pre-party activity, with one or two people playing various games while the remaining guests are arriving.

3. These homemade games are especially usable on a rainy day, or by children while convalescing.

4. Such games make excellent progressive game party equipment when set up in various rooms. Guests move from game to game in groups of four as you would in a foursome of golf.

Games You Can Make

RUBBER QUOITS

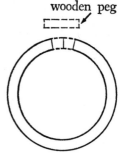

wooden peg

garden hose
24-30 inches long

Cut a piece of old garden hose 24 to 30 inches long. Then fashion a wooden peg to fit snugly into both ends of the hose. The game can be played like horseshoes with stakes in the ground. The distance is determined by the skill of the participants.

19

TETHERBALL

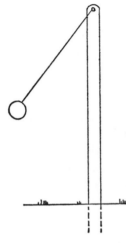

How to make: Get a section of 1¼-inch pipe 10 feet long. Get another section of pipe about 30 or 36 inches long and just large enough for the longer section of pipe to slip into. Drive the shorter piece of pipe into the ground so that it will be even with the surface; this will serve as a socket into which the long piece is set for play. If it is necessary to dismantle the game temporarily, the long piece may simply be lifted out of the socket and returned very easily. Drill holes in the top of the pipe for tying the rope. Take an old tennis ball or volleyball and cut two very small slits in it on opposite sides. The rope leading to the top of the pole may then be pushed through these slits and tied, but it is recommended that a piece of leather thong about 16 inches long be used to tie the ball to the rope. This will not wear out quite as easily as will regular clothesline rope.

How to play: Mark off the playing area into quadrants by means of two lines which intersect at the base of the pole and extent about 8 feet in each direction. Players take their positions in opposite quadrants and may not step out of their boundary lines. These boundary lines are important for safety's sake. The line on the post above which the ball must be wound should be about 6 feet from the ground. The game is started by one player hitting the ball with his hand or fist, either clockwise or counterclockwise. The opponent must hit the ball with a racket in the opposite direction. One point may be scored for the opponent each time that the ball hits the player on any part of his body except the forearm or hand holding the racket. Five points should be given for winding the ball up the pole. If the rope becomes wound around the arm of a player, his opponent is allowed a free swing at the ball when tossed.

Box Hockey

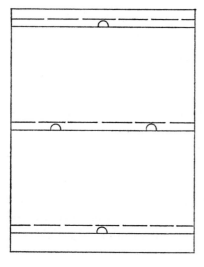

How to make: Using ordinary 2-inch pine wood, construct a sturdy box 6 feet long and 3 feet wide with sides about 10 inches high. Prepare two dividers which will fit in the box, and cut in the bottom of each a 6-inch square opening. Fit these dividers securely at either end of the box about 6 inches from each end wall. Prepare a third divider and cut in it two openings the same size as the end ones. Fit this divider securely in the middle of the box. Get several sections of old broomsticks. Take an old baseball bat and saw some cross sections smaller than the openings. You now have your hockey sticks and pucks and are ready to play.

How to play: The puck is placed on the top of the middle divider. Opponents, or teams of opponents, stand on either side of the box and face off with their sticks as in regular hockey. This is done by tapping the opponents' sticks and the bottom of the box three times in succession. After grounding the sticks the third time, the game is on. Each player tries to hit the puck through the opening in the end divider to his left. If the puck flies out of the box, it is put back into play by being dropped into the section of the box out of which it flew. No face-off is used in this case.

IMPROVISED BOCCIE

This is an Italian game which can be played by all ages. It is described in chapter 12 in "Backyard Activities."

Try-Your-Skill Games

The following descriptions and illustrations indicate the kind of games which can be developed with material found in the home. They may be used as informal activities or for a more organized event.

BASEBALL TILE TOSS

Equipment: 5 baseballs or tennis balls and 5 to 10 field tiles or weighted-down cans.

Setup: Stand tiles or cans on end and arrange in a pattern, such as a circle, line, square, or like bowling pins.

Object: Toss the ball into tiles or cans from some distance.

BALLOON IN BASKET

Equipment: A balloon and a clothes or bushel basket.

Setup: Place basket on floor or table.

Object: Shoot or toss balloon into basket from a line.

SET UP THE BOTTLE

Equipment: A pop bottle, rubber jar ring, 30-inch piece of string, and a stick.

Setup: Tie one end of string to jar ring and the other to stick. Lay bottle on its side.

Object: Set the bottle in an upright position, using the stick to manipulate the jar ring.

23

Drop the Clothespin

Equipment: A glass milk bottle or pint can and 5 clothespins.

Setup: Place the bottle on the floor.

Object: Drop a clothespin into bottle from chin height.

Ping-Pong Drop

Equipment: A quart jar and 5 ping-pong balls.

Setup: Place the jar on a table.

Object: Drop the ball into the jar from arm's length.

Ping-Pong Bounce

Equipment: A set of mixing bowls or dishes or pans of various sizes and 5 ping-pong balls.

Setup: Line up bowls on table or floor with a space between each. Assign scores to different size bowls.

Object: Stand back of a line and bounce balls into bowls.

Knock Down the Cans

Equipment: Tennis ball, bean bag or rubber ball, and 5 tin cans.

Setup: Place the cans on a bench or shelf. Mark different scores on the cans.

Object: Throw at the cans, trying to knock them over.

Bowl Down

Equipment: 5 or 10 tin cans and 2 softballs or tennis balls or rubber balls.

Setup: Set up cans like bowling pins or in some other pattern—line, circle, square, etc.

Object: Bowl the balls, trying to knock cans down.

Jerk and Catch

Equipment: Garbage can cover or pan lids, string, and a cloth or wad of paper.

Setup: Tie cloth to end of string. Lay it on the table. One player holds end of string and another player holds lid about 4 to 6 inches above cloth.

Object: Jerk the cloth out before the person with the lid can stop it.

No Eggs Please

Equipment: Several coins, slugs, ping-pong balls, or bottle caps, and an egg carton or muffin tin.

Setup: Place various scores in compartments of carton.

Object: Stand back of a line and toss coins or other things into carton.

The following party is one good way to use these skill games.

Carnival Night Party

Many of these games will be distributed about the room or yard. The number of games or "stations" will be determined by the amount of space provided in the home for this party. Guests will be divided into groups of two to four players. The games should be described to all guests before the play starts. A description of each game and the scoring is written on a card at each station. The leader indicates when the play starts, when the play stops, when scores are added up, and when players proceed to the next station. A number should be posted on each station in digits large enough to be readily seen.

Each person has a scorecard and records the score at the end of each game. Added interest can be achieved by having half of the group move clockwise and the other half move counterclockwise, and having the guests change partners at the end of each move.

3

FUN AT MEALTIMES

The family meal can be a very important center of family recreation. No matter how scattered the family is during most of the day, there is usually occasion for one or two meals together. These meals should be occasions of warm and jolly fellowship. However, in these days both the children and parents are involved in many community activities that prevent all the members from participating in relaxing conversation and activities during a leisurely meal. Perhaps one evening meal a week could be set aside, when all members are present and have time to share in activities around the table.

The suggestions in this chapter are pointed toward helping families to make mealtime a varied and interesting part of family life. Remember: mealtime is not a time for holding court. Scolding, teasing, punishing hinder digestion, but more than that, they spoil the pleasure and fellowship which a good meal can foster.

Outdoor Meal

At one time cooking over the open fire was a necessity. Man knew no other way. Now we do it for recreation. This form of meal preparation often becomes a necessity in times of local or national emergency. There are good outdoor cooking manuals available at libraries and bookstores.

The open fire should be prepared one or two hours before cooking time. Select hardwoods and allow two to three hours to burn down into cooking coals. Hickory and Osage orange wood are most desirable. Apple, linden, cherry, sycamore, oak, hackberry, and elm make suitable coals also. For satisfactory results, the bed of coals should be 4 to 6 inches deep.

Charcoal is gaining in popularity for outdoor cooking. It is faster—can be ready for cooking in 20 minutes. Directions for kindling are on the bag. It is easier to obtain and handle than wood.

Charcoal grills are fast outmoding the backyard fireplace in new communities. A simple and inexpensive fuel for outdoor cookery is corncobs.

Exercise Before Breakfast

Before breakfast, or anytime, have the family join in physical exercises. Have each member of the family lead one stretcher that he makes up himself. Everyone attempts to follow. The rule is to use nothing previously done.

Fun Around the Table

Table Conversation

Quotes, clippings, new riddles, and jokes are in order. These can be shared from newspapers, magazines, books, radio, and television.

Conundrums

Why is the letter "A" like noon? It is in the middle of "day." Men should avoid the letter "A" because it makes men mean. When is the letter "D" like a bad boy? When it makes ma mad. The merriest letter in the alphabet is "U" because it is in the middle of "fun." Which of mother's dresses last the longest? House dresses, because they are never worn out.

Riddles

How is an empty room like a roomful of married folks? Not a single person in it. What comes after "B" in "alphabet"? "E." Name me and you break me—silence. The difference between 16 ounces of butter and a pianist is? One weighs a pound and the other pounds away. How many more can you add?

Family History

"When mother was a girl" can be interesting table conversation if she tells about her good times and amusing experiences. A visit by grandma will help this theme along.

It is a satisfying thrill to have teen-agers and married children return home and suggest, "Let's go down to the old mill pond" (or some such place), like they used to. Those trips and excursions which parents endured were really enjoyed after all.

Relating family customs of the past may help further

29

the understanding and appreciation for contemporary living.

I Am Thinking

Someone starts by saying, "I am thinking of a ———" and others in turn discover what he is thinking about by asking questions that can be answered with yes or no.

Geography

Dad starts off by naming a river, country, state, city, body of water, island, mountain, or peninsula. The person on his right has to think of another geographical object that begins with the last letter of dad's word. Example:

Dad: Kansas
Mary: Salem
Tom: Montana
Mother: Amazon

Sound Waves for Supper

Strike the tines of a dinner fork on the edge of the plate and then hold them close to your ear. Hold vertically and twist slowly. Note the strange effect. Certain sound waves dim and grow loud as the fork is twisted. The external ear is not the only part of your body that hears. The bones of your head are also a sounding board. Strike the tines and then quickly and firmly touch the handle to the bone just behind the ear. Next, strike the tines and clamp the handle between your teeth.

Make a set of chimes with the water tumblers. Chords and melodies can be clanged out with spoon or fork as hammers. Tune the glasses by adding to or emptying out the water.

Tongue Twisters

Challenge someone to say one of the following three times—but quick!

1. Rugged rubber buggy bumpers.
2. Priscilla Prim plucks petunias.
3. Betty Blue blows big black bubbles.

Puzzlers

Try the following:

1. Count ten to one backwards.

2. If you were to go to bed at 7 P.M. and set your alarm for 8 A.M., how many hours sleep would you get?

3. How many months in the year have twenty-eight days?

4. Can you name a place where *you* can sit and I can't?

5. Pronounce h-i-g-h-e-r; h-u-g-h-e-r.

Answers:

1. 1-2-3-4-5-6-7-8-9-10.

2. One hour. Clocks cannot differentiate between A.M. and P.M.

3. Twelve.

4. My lap.

5. Higher. Hug her.

Repeat

Challenge someone to read once, and repeat twice with speed: "Good morning, Madam," to Eve said Adam. "Good morning, Adam," to him said she.

Mathematical Curiosities

Figures often play pranks. Note the following freak mathematical results:

$$1 \text{ times } 9 \text{ plus } 2 \text{ equals} \ldots \quad 11$$
$$12 \text{ times } 9 \text{ plus } 3 \text{ equals} \ldots \quad 111$$
$$123 \text{ times } 9 \text{ plus } 4 \text{ equals} \ldots \quad 1111$$
$$1{,}234 \text{ times } 9 \text{ plus } 5 \text{ equals} \ldots 11111$$

Continue to figure in this same manner on up to 12,345,678. You will find that this number times 9 plus 9 equals 111,111,111.

Joke Night

Let it be understood in the family that one night during each week will be joke night. Each member of the family will be responsible for sharing at least one joke with the rest of the family as they are seated about the table. Members of the family will be encouraged to do research during the week in magazines, joke books, newspapers, personal interviews, and any other sources of new jokes to share with the family. Younger children may be given some help by other members of the family. A variation could be introduced by occasionally making "joke night" conundrum night.

Hidden Conundrums

Before the family gathers at the table for a meal, someone places conundrums or questions under each plate. At a certain point in the meal someone says, "Dad, look under your plate." He pulls out the card and reads it. Everyone works on the problem. Then another person looks under his plate and another puzzle is worked. Answers are on the back of the cards.

Table Sentence Builder

One person starts and each person around the circle to the left adds a word until the sentence is finished. There is no penalty for finishing a sentence, but the next person on the left starts a new sentence with a new word.

Rhymes

For a meal game, rhymes can sometimes be used. Each person who can add one, does. "I see a bear." "Oh, tell me where!" "Under the chair." "Does he have any hair?"

Guessing Games

Some object can be described. Or, "I'm thinking of something that's round and white . . . with black numbers . . . and things that move. . . ." A guess is allowed between each clue.

Up, Jenkins

Players on one side of table are one team; those on the other side, the other team. One team gets a coin and passes it from player to player. The leader of the opposite team says, "Up, Jenkins!" and all hands are slapped down on the table with palms spread out, resting on table. Opposite team guesses which hand covers coin.

Table Stunt—Anvil Chorus

Let someone click the rhythm of a song on his glass. As others recognize the song, they sing it.

Napkin Problem

Especially for table fun. The problem: to tie a knot in a napkin without letting go of the ends. The answer: fold arms on chest, bend over napkin on table with arms still folded, take hold of ends, then unfold arms.

4

FAMILY BIRTHDAY PARTIES

Birthdays are days of celebration. Gifts, a special treat, dinner out, or a few friends asked to join the event are typical ways of observing the birthdays of young people and adults. Within the family circle, a birthday calls for special attention by all. Special ceremonies or rituals can be developed of a semi-serious and of a humorous nature identifying the significance of the particular age celebrated. These might be developed as an induction or "oath taking" into a new age, such as is done in some of the Indian tribes as a boy moves from youth to manhood.

The various growth periods can be identified as having family significance and being worthy of special recognition. Note the following list:

1. Six years—beginning of school life.

2. Eight years—now member of Brownies, Cub Scouts, or Indian Guides in YMCA.

3. Ten years—two-digit age; member of 4-H Clubs.

4. Thirteen years—a teen-ager with Social Security number.

5. Sixteen years—right to work without permit; can drive a car.

6. Nineteen years—no more income tax deductions.

7. Twenty-one—right to vote and become a responsible citizen.

Some families find a birthday an occasion for taking a photograph of the one whose birthday is being celebrated, or permitting him or her to make a special telephone call to some distant friend or relative. Another pattern that has charm is to send greeting cards on this day to other friends.

At the dinner table on the day of celebration the conversation may well lead to the family sharing previous family birthdays, recalling where they were and what they did. Here is the occasion for a poetic tribute or a musical parody to the member being honored or to have a few neighbors or friends drop in for dessert.

Some Party Suggestions

PARTIES FOR CHILDREN

Costume Party.
Mother Goose Supper.
Tepee Pow Wows for Little Children.

Hints:

1. Be sure to plan it with the child, not for him.
2. Make the party gay and festive with colorful decorations, funny paper hats, balloons, and favors for each child.
3. Have child select the friends to be invited.

4. Have child assist in writing the invitations.
5. Child should be at the door to receive each guest and to personally receive each gift.
6. Mother should be sure each gift is marked with the giver's name so he can be thanked for it.
7. Even though the giver may want the child to open the gift at once, place them all together and plan the opening of the gifts as part of the program later.
8. Do not overorganize a party for younger children.
9. At the start, have toys on the floor that youngsters can play with in an easy, relaxed manner when they first arrive. Example: a clothesline on the floor arranged like a highway, with a cloverleaf, bridges, tunnels, and four to six small cars, will occupy four or five children in play and conversation for quite a while.
10. When the party is for younger children, be sure to wrap up cake, cookies, or candies for them to take home. Each child needs something tangible to take home to show his family he was at a birthday party.

Parties for Teen-agers

On the Go! Arrange for attendance at a sports event or a roller skating rink.

Our Hero. Costume party—everyone wears apparel of a favorite hero.

PARTIES FOR ADULTS

A Man's World—all men's supper.
A Night at the Opera—for music lovers.
Hawaiian Feast.

Games and Events for All Ages

BALLOON BALL

The group is lined up in two lines facing each other. They must stay in their line as they try to hit the balloon across the line behind the other group. The side that bats the balloon across first wins.

BALLOON SWAT

Played as Balloon Ball except that players are seated and must keep one hand on their chair at all times.

LARGEST BALLOON

Give each person a balloon, preferably the same kind and size. On the signal "Go," each person starts blowing up his balloon. After a certain time limit, the largest unbroken balloon wins. Before the leader says "Go," it's a good idea to tell the contestants how long they have to blow their balloons.

GUESS THE LEADER

Have everyone seated in a circle, in chairs or on the floor. Choose one person to be "It." Have "It" leave the room. Choose one person in the circle for the leader. When "It" returns, everyone begins to clap. "It" stands in the middle of the circle or moves around, trying to discover who's the leader. The leader changes motions as quickly as he can without being caught. Some motions are: tapping the floor, shaking a finger, waving a hand. Everyone in the circle follows the leader and changes motions as he changes. When "It" discovers who is leader, the leader becomes "It" and goes outside. The group then chooses another leader.

A Hunt by Music

Let one person be "It" and leave the room. Have the group hide a small object such as a comb or a key case and choose a familiar song to sing, for example, "She'll be coming round the mountain." Call "It" back into the room. "It" searches for the object while the group sings. The group sings softly when "It" is far away from the object. Singing gets louder as "It" gets nearer the object, and the singing is very loud as "It" gets closer and closer. A yell or two adds zest. When "It" finds the object, he chooses another person as "It." If the object is hidden on or about a person, that person becomes "It" when the object is found.

Articles from Purse and Pocket

Divide into teams of five or more, depending on the size of the group. Appoint a leader for each team. Give each leader a list of articles which might be found in the purses or pockets of the team members. On the signal, have each team begin assembling the articles on its list. The team that first collects all the articles wins. Or, after a specific time, the group that has assembled the most articles from the list wins. The list of articles might include: white comb, stick of chlorophyll gum, 1945 penny, Social Security card, brown billfold, tube of bright red lipstick, nail file, hunting and fishing license, pocketknife.

FAMILY CONCERT

Have the group seated. See that each person has a glass of water and a spoon. The group may sing a familiar (2/4 or 4/4 time) song; keep time to the piano or a record. For the first eight beats, everyone taps on the water glass with a spoon. For the second eight beats, everyone taps on the table. For the third eight beats, everyone claps. For the fourth eight beats, everyone whistles the tune. Let the group continue to repeat the order until they have gone through the song twice. Direct in formal style, if you wish, with flourishes and gestures for fun.

WRITING BY MAGIC

Have one player, who knows the stunt, claim to be a magician and leave the room. Let the group choose any word. Call in the magician and have his partner ("secret" partner, as the group does not know that he is in on the stunt) go through the pretense of writing on the floor with a stick or cane. The scratches and flourishes the writer makes are of no interest to the magician, who is listening to the sentences and to the taps his partner is making in spelling out the chosen word. One tap means *a;* two taps mean *e;* three taps mean *i;* four taps mean *o;* and five taps mean *u*—all the vowels. The writer indicates the consonants by using them in their proper order as the first words of short sentences. For example, *cat* may be spelled in this way: the writer says, "Can you read this?" to indicate the letter *c,* while he moves the stick around; then he gives one tap for *a;* then he says, "This isn't easy," to indicate the letter *t.*

LIGHTS OUT (*for teen-agers and adults only*)

The object of this game is to light a match in one stroke and blow it out in one blow. The winner is the one who can light and blow out the most matches in a minute. Use only wooden matches.

INDOOR SCAVENGER HUNT

Prepare a list of items which are hidden inside the house or in designated rooms. Dresser drawers and cabinets are out of bounds. The list can include items such as: a February 1965 newspaper, an old medicine bottle, a 1964 calendar, etc. Conduct the hunt by couples. Limit the time for finishing the hunt.

CAR LOT

The purpose of this game is to see who can list the names of the most automobiles, old or new. Provide guests with paper and pencil. A time limit is set.

5

HOLIDAYS TOGETHER

The special days of the year can give purpose and direction to family activities. Whether it be a day free from work or just a day honoring some person or event, it should be a day for reviving traditions and customs and providing a memorable occasion for every member of the family.

As the time for celebration of this special day approaches, one member of the family should be asked to secure and read aloud the history and meaning of this day. This should be the time for creative planning on new ways of observing it. One family may decide to make it just a family event around the dinner table, while another will want to invite others to share in a group family party, or plan a visit to members of the family in other cities.

Whatever the decision is, planning together, involving all members of the family from the very beginning, is basic to family enjoyment. Everyone's idea is worth considering, and everyone shares in the responsibilities of the event.

The following are suggested ways of observing some of the special days of the year.

New Year's Day

All the family will want to sleep late, because everyone has been up late watching in the New Year. Because of this, a family "brunch" about midmorning would be a fine time to invite a few neighborhood families to enjoy the first day of the new year.

Following the meal is a time for a few activities:

Postcard Passing Relay

Divide group into teams. Four postcards are used for each team. The starter passes the first postcard by placing it between the fingers of the second person's left hand. The second person then places it between the fingers of his right hand, and places it with that hand between the fingers of the third person's left hand, etc. As soon as the first postcard has left the first person's hand, the second one is started. The game continues in this manner until all the postcards have returned to the starter. If a player drops one of the postcards, that card must be started over again with the first person.

Chair Relay

Divide group into two or more teams lined up in couples. Each couple links elbows. Each team has a chair (folding chair is best). The first couple carries the chair to the goal, puts it down. The boy seats the girl, she gets up, then they race back with the chair and the next couple starts. At all times the elbows of each couple must remain linked.

Coin Relay

Divide group into teams. First person from each team places a coin on the back of his hand. He then moves a distance of about two to three feet from the second person. He tosses the coin to the second player. The second player must then catch the coin on the back of his hand. The coin is passed on until each person has had a turn.

Valentine's Day

This is the day for sweethearts to share friendship with others, and it calls for a party. It may be a children's party or a party for married couples. All members of the family help decorate the home with hearts, arrows, cupids, and comic valentines, and share in preparing and serving the refreshments.

The following activities would be appropriate for a party for either young or old:

Valentine Word Builders

Compete by groups to see how many different words can be developed out of words like "matrimony," "valentine," "romance," "courtship."

Valentine Telegram

Give each person a card on which the letters V-A-L-E-N-T-I-N-E are written down the left side. Each person writes a telegram using each letter in the word "valentine" as the first letter of each word, respectively.

Easter

This is the day the entire family attends church together. This might also be the day to invite to an Easter dinner a family new to the community or some family that might be alone because all their relatives live far away. It will give everybody a chance to become acquainted and to form new friendships. The family chosen should have children of corresponding ages with your family if at all possible.

When younger children are in the family, the coloring and decorating of the eggs is an enjoyable family enterprise. These are then hidden around the room and used for an egg hunt following dinner.

Decorated baskets full of chocolate eggs can be an appropriate Easter gift for all the children.

Reading the Bible story and other Easter stories will make good conversation around the dinner table. Having the older members recall Easters of the past will promote interesting talks and questions.

Fourth of July

A holiday from work and school makes this day ideal for a trip somewhere—to visit friends or relatives or some spot of historic or scenic interest. Make it a leisurely trip with stops en route.

Planning for the trip can make it an expedition instead of travel just to get somewhere. Deciding on the time to start, the road to be taken, and stops en route should be a family decision. This is much easier to do if you leave plenty of time for going and coming. Visiting spots of interest can be a fine way of enlarging one's knowledge of the history of our country.

This trip could be the start of a logbook of your family travels noting distances, places of interest, names of restaurants, and people met. If photography is the hobby of a member of the family, pictures taken on the trip will add much to the log.

Labor Day

Labor day is another whole day free from work and school. It's harvest time with sweet corn, tomatoes, and other vegetables and fruits aplenty. This calls for an outdoor barbecue, hamburger or wienie roast with some friends, neighbors, or relatives. Have the children each invite a special friend.

If your guests are intimate friends, they might prefer making it a "pot luck" with each family providing a part of the dinner. This adds much to the feeling of friendliness, for all have shared in making this event possible.

Before and after dinner, have several pieces of outdoor equipment available, such as croquet, badminton, rubber quoits, and tetherball. A family lawn game favorite is boccie ball, a form of lawn bowling (see chapter 12).

Halloween

Halloween is party time. Why not make it an evening full of games and events?

Bean Pitching

This game requires a small bowl, a medium-sized bowl, a dishpan, and beans. The small bowl is placed in the center of the larger bowl, and the larger bowl is placed inside the dishpan. The beans are tossed into these receptacles. Score five points for the small bowl, three points for the larger bowl, and one point for the dishpan. The player with the highest score gets a prize.

Ghost Snap

Bring into the room, one at a time, blindfolded players and ask them to walk directly up to a cardboard ghost on the wall and place a finger in the ghost's mouth. An accomplice, standing close by, puts a toy snapper on the extended finger. The blindfolded person, feeling his finger snapped, usually reacts in a comical way.

Pumpkin Hunt

Cut out small cardboard pumpkins and hide them around the room among the cornstalks. As each pumpkin is found, it may be redeemed for three beans. When all pumpkins are found, the one with the most beans wins.

Customary Partners

If you want your group divided into couples, try "Pork and Bean Partners." Each boy takes a slip of paper out of a "partner box"; the girls take their slips of paper out of a separate box. On these different slips of paper have been written the names of foods that invariably go together. After everyone has his slip of paper, Mr. Pork goes to find Miss Bean, Mr. Bread looks for Miss Butter, Mr. Liver for Miss Onion, etc.

ELIMINATION

Divide group into small teams. Each team is given a balloon. Each team starts by hitting its balloon into the air and attempts to keep it there. When a team's balloon touches the floor or some object in the room, that team is disqualified. The team that keeps its balloon airborne the longest, wins.

STICK UP BALLOON

Rub an inflated balloon against your clothing, preferably a rough surface like corduroy, and place it against a wall or ceiling. Usually it will stick. To make a game out of it, have everyone rub their balloons and put them on the wall. The balloon that sticks or stays up the longest, wins.

BLACK CAT DARTS

Draw and cut out a large black cat on heavy paper. Give each part of the cat a certain value. Each guest throws five darts at the cat, then his score is totaled.

TEARABLE ART

Give each player a piece of paper, all pieces being of equal size. Have the players hold the paper behind their backs and tear a simple object representing the time of the year or a national holiday. The players cannot look at the work of art until they have finished tearing. Display the "Tearable Art."

KEEN EYES

Players stand in two lines, one line facing the other. Each person observes closely what the person across from him is wearing. One line turns around and the other line is given a minute to make some changes in costume with another player on the team. (Untie a shoelace, turn a belt around or change rings.) The first team turns back and each player in turn down the line tries to guess what change was made by the person directly across from him. Score one point for each correct guess.

Thanksgiving

Thanksgiving dinner with immediate family and relatives is an American tradition. Mother will make sure that it will be a wonderful meal, but other members of the family can contribute significantly to this dinner by caring for other responsibilities:

1. Place cards can be unique and different. Have first names spelled backwards; or instead of names, write a compliment or a brief description of each person, or just have their birth date in place of a name.

2. Candy or nut cups can be decorated and prepared by someone other than mother.

3. Another member of the family can be responsible

for conversation topics of interest, such as having Aunt Jennie describe her first Thanksgiving dinner, or Uncle Charley describe his hunting of rabbit or wild turkey. Take turns describing earliest recollections as a child. It's always good family fun to have the older members of the family describe some early childhood experiences, though they may seem unbelievable to the younger generation.

Christmas

This is the day for the family to enjoy each other in the intimate family group. The home at Christmas is the symbol of peace and openhearted living for which the world so wistfully seeks. Each family can make it more meaningful by discussing the meaning of Christmas and by reading aloud such stories as "The Night Before Christmas," Dicken's "Christmas Carol," or Henry van Dyke's "Keep Christmas." It should also be a time for singing together the familiar Christmas carols.

The exchanging of gifts is of much importance in every family, so why not make the most of it by adding a few new ways of receiving and giving the gifts? Here are a few suggestions:

1. Allow plenty of time for each person to open his gift, identify the giver, and show it to other members of the family before opening another gift.

2. Have each member of the family take turns going to the tree, picking out a gift, and giving it to the proper person.

3. Hide some gifts around the room, connecting them to the tree by means of long pieces of string with name tags attached. The recipient must find his gift by following the string.

4. Have each person make five guesses as to the contents before opening his package.

5. Save one unopened gift for the day after Christmas. This element of suspense will add another day to the Christmas spirit.

JINGLE BELLS

The old game of Reuben and Rachel is played with a new twist. The players form a circle around one couple. The boy in the center is blindfolded, and the girl has several sleigh bells hanging around her neck or arm. The purpose of the game is for the boy to catch the girl. When the boy calls "Jingle," the girl must make the bells ring. He may call as often as he wishes, and it will take a fleet-footed female to keep out of his way.

CHRISTMAS BLUFF

The player who is chosen for Santa Claus stands in the center of the room blindfolded, with the other players (Santa's reindeer) scattered around him. Each reindeer has a jingle bell on a string around his neck which guides Santa in finding him. Santa walks around trying to find his reindeer. When he catches one, he guesses who it is. If the guess is correct, the two exchange places.

SNOWSTORM

Contestants line up in relay formation. Each player is provided with a downy snow-white feather. At a signal, the first player blows his feather toward the goal line. It may be necessary for the contestants to get down on their hands and knees if their feathers should drop to the floor.

6
TEEN-AGE PARTIES AT HOME

The period of adolescence is a relatively short but turbulent spasm in the stages of family living. Recreation activities in the home can be a way of letting off steam, forming friendships, accepting responsibility, and developing the skill of being a good host.

The home should be the place where the teen-ager brings his friends, and where parties are the occasions for groups of friends to gather.

Teen age is the time of life for youngsters to express themselves on areas of life which will be a part of their future. Serious or humorous discussion can be a part of a social evening on such topics as "the kind of college or university I want to attend; the kind of job I want to have ten years from now; or the kind of woman or man I want to marry."

Many teen-age parties today consist of playing records, games, and plenty of soft drinks and food. The creative individual will add the possibility of dramatic skits, charades, stunts, relays, and physical activities.

The party theme can determine the party invitation, the decorations, program, and costumes. The following are the names of teen-age parties which can be the themes around which the total event revolves: Back to School; College Daze; Vacation Plus; Fall Barbeque Binge; Western Party; Ski and Skating Frolic; Treasure Island; Come as Sloppy as You Can; Shipwreck Party; Famous Couples; and a Christmas Caroling Party.

Fun in the Kitchen

All the guests have a chance to share in the "party." (Draw straws or numbers for certain tasks or jobs.)
The kitchen:

1. The crowd shares the responsibility of keeping the kitchen clean.
2. Appearance should be bright and pleasant.
3. Plenty of pans, glasses, and dishes.
4. Table and chairs—either in kitchen or nearby.

Keep pantry and refrigerator well stocked. (Teen-agers enjoy hardy food which is easy to prepare. Substitutions are encouraged.)

1. Eggs and bacon.
2. Cokes, fruit juices, milk, cocoa.
3. Cheeses, cold meat, roast.
4. Bread, cakes, cookies.
5. Lettuce, onions, mustard, relishes.
6. Pizza mixes.
7. Napkins.

Other possibilities:

1. Nuts, apples, popcorn around the fire.
2. Outside fireplace cooking, especially in the fall. Hot

dogs, baked potatoes, corn on the cob, hamburgers, or sloppy Joes after football games.

Drop-in Parties

Parents have the opportunity to magnify the feeling of this is "our" party for teen-agers by being ready to help when asked. This help should be given ahead of time if the teen-ager is to do a good job. The recreation room, living room, lawn, or porch may provide for the drop-in as well as the planned and organized party. The rest of this chapter suggests games, activities, and relays that may be a part of the program.

At an agreed-upon time in the party, father and mother appear dressed as waiter and waitress to serve the refreshments.

Pairing Up

PARTNER DESCRIPTIONS

All draw numbers, those of the girls corresponding with those of the boys. The first fellow calls his number, and praises his unknown partner by telling her what he thinks is the loveliest thing about her. When he has finished, his partner steps out and is identified, and the two go to the side. This continues until everyone has a partner.

FISHING FOR PARTNERS

A curtain is stretched over a doorway with an opening of about a foot above it. Small fishing poles (about three) with bent hooks are given to either the boys or girls, who fish for their partners. The fishing consists of throwing the line over the top of the curtain, while the leader puts a name slip on each hook.

Trip to the Moon

Two sets of chairs are arranged in a double line, chairs back to back. Boys form a circle around one set, girls around the other. In each there is one fewer chair than there are persons. As the music starts, the players march around chairs; when it stops, each tries to sit on a chair. The girl and boy left out become partners for the next event. Each removes a chair from the circles, and the game continues until all have partners.

Slip Spy

The girls write their names on slips of paper when they arrive. While the guests are busy with something else, someone hides the names in easy-to-find places, preferably in another room. The boys hunt for the names, stopping after they find one name.

Singing Partners

The names of familiar songs are written on duplicate slips. One slip is given to a boy and the other to a girl. At a signal from the leader or hostess, all start singing or whistling their songs. This mixer will create a lot of noise as well as fun. When partners are found, the singing stops.

PARTNER RACE

Have each person write his name backwards on a slip of paper. (Mary Smith becomes Htims Yram.) Pass out the girls' slips of paper to the boys; and at a given signal, let all the boys read the slips, find their partners, and hold hands high.

Relays

MATCHBOX RELAY

Provide each team with the outside of a safety matchbox. At the starting signal, the box is put on number 1's nose, who in turn passes it from his nose to number 2's nose without using his hands. If the matchbox falls to the floor, it must go back on the nose of the person who dropped it before it can be passed on to the next person. This game is fun for onlookers as well as for good competition.

In playing relays, see that teams or sides line up boy, girl, boy, girl, all the way down the line.

ORANGE OR GRAPEFRUIT RELAY

Provide each team with an orange. At the starting signal, the orange is placed under number 1's chin. He faces the next player in line and passes it on to her so that she gets it firmly under her chin, *without the use of hands.* Players cooperate in passing the orange from one to the next, but no hands may assist in the transfer.

Hands are used to rescue the oranges that have fallen to the floor.

Ring and Toothpick

Provide each player with a toothpick. Each team is given a ring. At the starting signal, each player places the toothpick in his mouth. The first player places the ring on his toothpick and transfers it to the next player's toothpick without the use of hands.

Chewing Gum Relay

Give each team a ladies' handbag in which there is a small folded paper bag and inside of that several fully wrapped sticks of gum. The first person is handed a pair of canvas gloves. On a signal this person puts on the gloves, opens the bag and gets one stick of the chewing gum, chews it and whistles before passing on the bag to the next person, who repeats the pattern.

Ping-pong Relay

Arrange two teams of couples. The head couple is given a ping-pong ball. On a signal they support the ball between their foreheads with their hands on each other's shoulders. They walk to the end of the room and return to give the ball to the next couple in line.

Games

Ping-Pong Polo

Gather two teams around a table. The team players alternate positions about the table. One team defends one half of the table and one team the other. All players kneel or squat down so that their chins rest on the edge of the table. A ping-pong ball is placed at the center of the table. At a starting signal, the players try to blow the ball off the table on the opponent's side. The chins may not be lifted from the table once the ball is put in play. Play several innings.

THREE JEALOUS LOVERS

An imaginary flooded stream crosses the room. Three couples are on one side of the stream trying to find a way to cross. They have obtained a boat from upstream, but it holds only two people. The problem is to get all six people across without one fellow being alone with another fellow's partner on either side of the stream. All six can row, but the fellows are so jealous that they will not permit their dates to be with another fellow. How can these six people cross the stream without any girl being found in the company of either or both of the other fellows without her date being present?

Use a rug or mark on the floor to represent the stream. Have six chairs on either side of the rug or mark. The couples move across the rug in accordance with the above conditions.

One solution:
    Couple 1 crosses.
    Boy 1 returns.
    Girls 2 and 3 cross.
    Girl 1 returns.

Boys 2 and 3 cross.
Couple 2 returns.
Boys 1 and 2 cross.
Girl 3 returns.
Girls 1 and 2 cross.
Boy 3 returns.
Couple 3 crosses.

HUNTER, FOX, AND GUN

Two lines of players stand on opposite sides of the room facing each other. The head player of each line decides whether the line shall represent hunters, foxes, or guns. Then each runs down his line, whispering this information to the players. The leaders stay at the foot of the lines, so that for the next inning each line will have a new head.

At a signal each line walks forward three steps, falls into position, and makes the noise of the object it is representing. If the players are hunters, they stand with hands on hips and say "Hep!" If they are guns, they pretend to shoot a gun and say "Bang!" If they are foxes, they put their thumbs in their ears, wave their fingers at the other line, and cry "Yip, yip, yip!"

Points are scored on the following basis: foxes defeat hunters, hunters defeat guns, and guns defeat foxes. For example, if one team has chosen to represent foxes and the opposing team represents hunters, a point is awarded to the foxes. But if one team represents foxes and the opposing team represents guns, the foxes lose the point. If both teams represent the same thing, neither one scores. Ten points are a game, but five points may be enough if there are many ties.

HUMAN CHECKERS

Place seven chairs in a row and seat three boys and three girls as indicated: B-B-B-O-G-G-G. Have each group of six players choose a captain or director. The object of the game is for the captain to move the boys and girls to opposite seats, like checkers, moving or jumping one at a time. No player may be moved backwards. All may be started over again if they get stuck. The final result will be G-G-G-O-B-B-B. If there are but six players, this may be done against time.

Help for the Captain: After the first player is moved, do not let two players on the same side get together. Solution:

B-B-B-O-G-G-G

B-B-O-B-G-G-G

B-B-G-B-O-G-G

B-B-G-B-G-O-G

B-B-G-O-G-B-G

B-O-G-B-G-B-G

O-B-G-B-G-B-G

G-B-O-B-G-B-G

G-B-G-B-O-B-G

G-B-G-B-G-B-O

G-B-G-B-G-O-B

G-B-G-O-G-B-B

G-O-G-B-G-B-B

G-G-O-B-G-B-B
G-G-G-B-O-B-B
G-G-G-O-B-B-B

Human Ticktacktoe

Make a large ticktacktoe pattern on the floor between two teams, or arrange nine chairs in three rows of three chairs each. Then play ticktacktoe, using team members as markers. Each team tries to place three members in a row.

One player at a time from each side, in rotation, steps into a square or sits in a chair. When three players from the same team sit in a row, they score for their side and win that inning. Permit no coaching during play. Players must keep in mind who are their team members and which are opponents while moving to get three in a row or preventing the opponents from doing the same.

Call Another

Seat players in a line or circle. Have them number off, starting with number 1. The chairs in which the players are seated retain the original numbers throughout the game. As the players change chairs, each player takes the number of the chair he now occupies.

The highest number starts by calling another number. Each person who is called calls another number. For example, the highest number may call 5; then 5 must respond by calling another. When a person whose number is called does not respond immediately, he must go to the foot. All players below him move up one space and change their numbers. Thus, player 6 becomes player 5; player 5 becomes player 4; and so on down the line. Players call numbers rapidly and make a special effort to send the top players to the foot.

Any player who speaks out of turn, stutters, or waits too long to respond must go to the foot. This can be played in rhythm. The group may use this rhythm pattern: clap hands, clap knees, snap fingers. The number is called on the snap of the fingers.

Comical Track Meet

Events in an indoor track meet are shot put (with a balloon), javelin throw (with a paper dart), the standing long whistle, the standing broad grin, and the half-yard dash (won by the longest foot).

Balloon Stick

A sizable box or wastebasket is placed in the middle of the floor. At equal distances from it, on opposite sides, are balloons. Behind each balloon stands a player with a stick. On signal, each player, using only his stick, tries to guide his balloon into the wastebasket.

Card Toss

From a fixed distance, each player tries to flick or soar ten cards into a bucket or wastebasket. The first to score twenty-one wins.

Drop the Penny

A quarter is placed in a bucket of water on the floor. Players standing erect try to drop pennies so that they will lie on the quarter. The first to succeed wins.

Beauty Contest

Each girl is given plenty of newspaper, pins, lipstick, face powder, bobby pins, and ribbon. With a boy as a model, she dresses him up as a girl and enters him in a beauty contest.

Predicaments

A boy and girl are asked to leave the room. While they are out, all persons in the group agree on a predicament, such as "the house is on fire," or "locked out of my house," or "lost in a storm," or "lost the key to the car." When the couple is asked to come back in, they are told to try to determine the chosen predicament by asking anyone, "What would you do?" The person asked gives an answer having the predicament in mind. The answers should not be so obvious that they give the predicament away at once.

Spell Down

Line up the teams for an old-fashioned spelling bee; of course, they spell the words backwards. It goes faster if the words are only five or six letters long and you have a thirty-second time limit. When anyone misses a word, send him to the foot of the class. After ten minutes, announce that the one at the foot of the class in backwards spelling must be the winner, and give him a candy bar as a prize to end the game.

ANIMALS

Players form a circle. Leader announces that he will give each player the name of an animal and that there will be two players with the same name. He places an apple in the center of the ring. Those whose names are called are to see who can grab the apple first. Actually, the name "monkey" has been given to every player; and when "monkey" is called, all dash for the apple.

OBSTACLE RACE

Arrange stacks of books or other nonbreakable objects on the floor about three feet apart. These are the obstacles. Place a raw egg between every other pair of obstacles for all to see. Blindfold a few players and start them walking toward the goal, telling them to be sure not to step on the eggs. After they have been blindfolded, remove all but one or two obstacles, and substitute soda crackers for the eggs. The crunching sound will be fatal.

CAN YOU FOLLOW DIRECTIONS?

The punch line is No. 19. Inform the participants that they have only three minutes to complete the quiz. Give everyone a copy of the following quiz:

1. Read everything before doing anything.
2. Put your name in the upper right-hand corner of this paper.
3. Circle the word "name" in sentence two.
4. Draw five small squares in the upper left-hand corner of this paper.
5. Put an "X" in each square.
6. Put a circle around each square.
7. Sign your name under the title.
8. After the title write "Yes, Yes, Yes."
9. Put a circle around each word in sentence No. 7.
10. Put an "X" in the lower left-hand corner of this paper.
11. Draw a triangle around the "X" you just put down.
12. On the reverse side of this paper multiply 703 by 9,805.
13. Draw a rectangle around the word "paper" in sentence No. 4.
14. Call out your first name when you get to this point in the test.
15. If you think you have followed the directions up to this point, call out "I have."
16. On the reverse side of this paper, add 8,950 and 9,850.
17. Put a circle around your answer. Put a square around the circle.
18. Count out loud in your normal voice backwards from ten to one.
19. Now that you have finished reading carefully, do only sentences one and two.

Terms in Baseball

Match the columns:

1. A summer pest	a. Ball
2. Hosiery bugbears	b. Sacrifice
3. Inaccurate	c. Homer
4. Holiday dinner	d. Bat
5. A successful effort	e. Fan
6. Vessel for pouring	f. Fly
7. Used for pancakes	g. Out
8. A good foundation	h. Plate
9. To take unlawfully	i. Foul
10. A flying visit	j. Shortstop
11. A dinner necessity	k. Base
12. If you forget your door key	l. Double
13. A disguise	m. Single
14. Dispenses judgment	n. Run
15. Proprietor of dog pound	o. Error
16. A coveted jewel	p. Catcher
17. Given for charity	q. Steal
18. Dangerous on highways	r. Fake
19. An offering	s. Batter
20. To multiply by 2	t. Pitcher
21. It flies only at night	u. Umpire
22. Unmarried	v. Diamond
23. A famous Greek poet	w. Shortstop
24. Used to gain relief in hot weather	x. Hit

Do This and Add Something

The group is seated in a small circle. The leader stands in the center, points to a player and makes a motion or says something. The player stands, repeats the motion or statement and adds another. The third player repeats the two motions or statements and adds a third. The game is thus continued around the circle.

Odd or Even?

Each player is given a definite number of beans which he holds in his closed palm. He places one or more beans in his other hand, approaches another player, and asks, "Odd or even?" If the second player guesses correctly, the first player loses a bean. In case the second player guesses incorrectly, the first player wins a bean.

Double Handcuff

This game requires two lengths of string about 2 to 3 feet long. At each end of both strings, make a loop with a slipknot.

After crossing the strings in the center, two players slip the loops onto their wrists. They are then told to separate themselves without untying any knots, breaking the string, or slipping their hands through the loops around their own wrists.

Solution: One person takes hold of string connecting partner's hands, slips it under the string around his own wrist and out over his own hand.

Name the States

Write down the names of the fifty states in five minutes. This is not as easy as it seems. A variation is to have the participants work in pairs.

Scrimmage

This is a game of impersonations in which the boys and girls form separate lines facing each other. First, the boys may impersonate book agents and try to sell the housewives a set of books. On signal the boys shift to different partners. Now the boys may be grocers and the girls housewives. The housewife received only eleven eggs in a carton and three of them were bad. The housewife gives the grocer a "calling down." Continue with other suggested impersonations.

Know the Players

Identify some of the guests by a name, a characteristic, an interesting fact, or an odd bit of clothing. Give a list like the following to each guest and have them all try to find and write in the name of the person described.

1. _____has tape on the temple of his glasses.
2. _____has the middle name Harold.
3. _____was born in December.
4. _____has an ankle chain on one ankle.
5. _____played football in high school.
6. _____has traveled in 15 states.

7. _____was born in Illinois.
8. _____is wearing a red tie.
9. _____has a hole in his sock.
10. _____is wearing two different socks.

Touch and Tell

Place several articles, perhaps ten, in a large sack. The leader carries the sack around to the players, each of whom is given thirty seconds to reach into the sack and feel the articles. Each person then from memory makes a list of things he thinks he touched. The winner is the person who has the longest correct listing.

Ocean Wave

Players are seated in *very sturdy chairs*. "It" is in the center. One chair is vacant. "It" calls, "Scoot right," and whoever is sitting to the left of the vacant chair quickly slides into it, and so on around the circle, each person scooting to his own right. "It" tries to sit in a vacant chair; if he is successful, the person who was supposed to slide into it becomes "It." "It" can call out at any time, "Scoot left," and the scooting reverses direction.

Find the Leader

The group is seated in a circle. "It" goes out of the room, and when he returns, he is to discover who is leading the group in crazy antics like waving feet, flapping ears, etc. "It" must go to the center of the circle and stay there, revolving about to see if he can tell who is starting these actions. When he is successful, that person becomes "It."

ELECTRIC SHOCK

Group stands in single circle, hands joined, one in center. A person in the group starts by saying, "I'm going to send a telegram to Mary Jones." Person in center turns his back for two to three seconds while the telegram gets started. (It passes from person to person by having hands squeezed. If you receive the squeeze on your left hand, you transmit it to your neighbor with your right hand.) The center person tries to discover where the "message" actually is. If he catches a player in the act of transmitting, that player becomes "It." If the telegram reaches the receiver successfully, "It" stays in the center again.

Folk Games

A few singing games and folk-game figures may be appropriate for the teen-age party. This type of activity is usually avoided because it seems difficult. Try the ones included here; and when you have learned the figures— which are really simpler than you would expect—introduce them at your school parties.

VIRGINIA REEL (simplified version)

Music: "Turkey in the Straw," "Pop Goes the Weasel," or "Miss McLeod's Reel."

Formation: Boys in one line, girls in the other. Partners are opposite each other.

Call	Action
Forward and bow	All partners take four steps toward each other, bow, and return. 8 counts.
Right hand round	Partners take right hands and swing. 8 counts.
Left hand round	Same with left hands. 8 counts.
Both hands swing	Partners grasp both hands and swing full turn. 8 counts.
Do-si-do	Players fold arms high, take four steps forward; partners go around each other, back to back, and then return to place with four backward steps.
Head couple reel	The head couple hooks right elbows, swings once and a half round. Unhook. Girl and second boy hook left elbows and swing round; meanwhile boy and second girl do same. The head couple returns to each other with right elbows and makes full turn; on to third boy and girl with left elbow; back to partner with right elbow again; and so on down to foot of set. Repeat with new head couple.

Skip to My Lou (Pennsylvania version)

Formation: Single circle of partners facing in, ladies to the right of the gentlemen. Extra players, if any, to the center; these obtain partners on step No. 8.

Words	*Action*
1. *Gents to the center,* skip to my Lou; Gents to the center, skip to my Lou; Gents to the center, skip to my Lou; Skip to my Lou, my darling.	1. Men to the center 8 steps and back (16 steps).
2. *Ladies to the center,* skip to my Lou; (Verse structure same as in No. 1, and continues for the next eight.)	2. Women to center and back (16 steps).
3. *Bow to your partner,* skip to my Lou; *Now to your opposite,* skip to my Lou; *Again to your partner,* skip to my Lou; Skip to my Lou, my darling.	3. Bow to each other as you sing. Bow to neighbor. Bow to partner again. Bow to neighbor again.
4. *Swing your partner,* etc.	4. Swing your partner twice around (16 steps).

5. *And now your opposite*, etc.

5. Swing lady on left twice around (16 steps).

6. *Promenade all and*, etc.

6. Promenade with partner (counter-clockwise).

7. *I lost my lover, what'll I do?* etc.

7. Ladies continue to march in the direction of the promenade. Men about-face and march clockwise.

8. *I found another one just as true;* etc.

8. Men about-face, seize a partner, and promenade as in No. 7. Extra players seize partners as well.

ADULT HOME PARTIES

Peer groups of all ages form the setting for meeting each other's needs. Adults also have needs which must be met. They need to associate with other adults, unencumbered by children. They have a need to form friends with other adults. Adult home parties provide the setting for the formation of new friendships and the fellowship of old friends.

Many adults have fears about social participation. Fears often block the fulfillment of needs and wants. "I don't know what they will do at the party, so we won't go." "I don't want to try anything new, because I don't want to risk making a mistake." Adults are critical of social activities they have never experienced. They do not like to be embarrassed. See that no one is embarrassed at your party!

Contemporary conversation on world events may be the theme of the evening. If the party can be held at a time when TV is presenting such a feature, view the program as a group, turn off the set, and launch out into a discussion of the implications of the situation.

Reading a play with guests taking different character

parts gives opportunity for being somebody else for a while.

Meet at someone's house early in the morning for a bird watch and breakfast.

Plan a planting party in March or April for the exchange of plants, shrubs, and perennials.

Get together to repair toys for children's homes and needy families.

Arrange for tours and trips through industrial plants, stores, and commercial establishments.

Rent or borrow bikes for a bike ride, horses for a trip on horseback, a bus for a bus trip, a boat for a boat trip.

Party Techniques and Games

The guests can be placed into groups by (1) counting off—if three teams by threes, if four teams by fours; number ones go into a group, twos into another, and so on; (2) birth dates—those whose birthdays are in (a) January, February, and March, (b) April, May, and June, (c) July, August, and September, (d) October, November, and December; (3) colored name tags or scorecards given each guest as he arrives.

CARNIVAL NIGHT

See chapter 2.

INDOOR TREASURE HUNT

Place the following items in places where they can be completely seen, but are not obvious. Have guests hunt in couples and urge them to check an article as soon as they see it, without informing other guests. Each couple is given a list of the items to be found.

Items: postage stamp, rubber band, paper clip, ladies' stocking (place between legs of a chair or hang in fold of drapery), man's necktie (on a table lamp), ping pong ball, dollar bill (on a book disguised as a title), golf tee, match, pencil, button, thumbtack.

CONVERSATION TOPICS

Inform the guests in advance of the topics to be discussed: favorite vacation spot, travel (indicating most traveled person during year), current news, favorite poems, quotations, cities of birth, wedding experiences, pet peeves, favorite economy.

BE AN ACTOR OR ARTIST

Divide the players into groups. Each group sends a representative to the leader, who gives a word or idea to be pantomimed or expressed in some way. Each representative hurries back to his own group and, using his ingenuity, tries to convey the idea to the group without telling them in words. The person who first guesses the correct answer wins a point for his group. Continue playing with a different member going to the leader each time. The group earning the most points wins.

Variation: Give the representative of each group a pencil and card with which he will draw a picture of the idea. The group that first guesses the idea from the picture wins.

CONSEQUENCES

At the leader's direction each person writes on a piece of paper an adjective describing a woman. Then he folds the paper about half an inch and passes it to the player on his right. Each player now writes a man's name, folds the paper again, and passes it on. This procedure is repeated until the following items are set down in order:

An adjective describing a woman	What he did
	What she said
A man's name	What he said
Where they met	The consequences
What she did	What the world said

The lists should be read aloud by either the leaders or the players. In reading the lists, words may be inserted to give continuity to the story.

CROSSED AND UNCROSSED

A pair of scissors is needed. Players are seated in a circle. Someone passes the scissors. That player passes them on saying, "I have received them crossed and pass them uncrossed." The crossed and uncrossed refer to the passer's legs or feet, though the uninitiated invariably think it has reference to the scissors. If the receiver's feet were crossed when the scissors are passed, and also crossed as he passes them, he says, "I received them crossed and pass them crossed."

Telegrams

Assign several letters to each player, letting him have five to ten minutes to work out a clever telegram, using these letters at the beginning of each word.

Guess the Number

Use pencil and paper, or make mental calculations. Ask someone to think of his age, the amount of change in his pocket, or any number up to 100. Tell him to multiply this number by 2, add 1, multiply by 5, add 5, multiply by 10, and tell you the result. You then take this number, subtract 10, drop the last 2 digits, and tell him the original number.

Teakettle

"It" leaves the room. Group chooses a word with many meanings. When "It" returns to the room, he will find the group using the word "teakettle" instead of the hidden word in sentences. He must guess what the hidden word is. (Use words with many meanings, like dear, deer; so, sew, sow; wear, where; etc.)

My Crazy Aunt

"My crazy aunt likes butter but she doesn't like meat." The aunt likes everything with double letters: butter, pepper, walls, etc., not jam, salt, ceilings. A person who knows this aunt and maybe an accomplice start talking about her. As others catch on, they join in the conversation.

The Cook's Questionnaire

Divide the group into teams. Leader reads statements and the team calling out the most correct answers first wins. The answer to each statement is in the form of some kind of cake.

The brightest cake	sunshine
The saint's cake	angel food
The cake that weighs the most	pound
The cake that weighs the least	feather
The hen's cake	layer
The cake with the royal title	Lady Baltimore
The cake that never pays its way	sponge
The variety cake	spice
The fire cake	hot
The squirrel's cake	nut
The fat woman's cake	jelly roll
The small boy's favorite	marble
The cake that is the farmer's delight	corn
The pep cake	ginger
The baby's cake	pat-a-cake
The cake that underweighs	shortcake
The tempter's cake	devil's food
The gardener's cake	hoecake
The football player's cake	griddle

Guessing

Have on a table pencils, paper, and some of the following:

A glass jar of beans (Guess how many.)
A large dictionary (What is the weight?)
A small ball of cord (How long?)
An apple or orange (How many seeds?)
One fourth of a page of a newspaper (How many words?)
A photo of a child or an animal (What is the age?)

TWENTY QUESTIONS

The player who is "It" thinks of some specific object anywhere in the world. By asking not more than twenty questions the other players try to learn what the object is. The questions must all be answered with "Yes" or "No" or "I don't know." Direct questions such as "Is it that door?" should be avoided until the group, by the process of elimination by general questions, feels pretty sure of the object.

WHAT IS AS . . . ?

The leader divides the players into two teams, each to compete against the other as anyone in either group calls out the answer immediately. Leader says, "Black as?" Answer—"Coal."

Red as? (Rose)
Green as? (Grass)
White as? (Snow)
Yellow as? (Butter)
Blue as? (Sky)
Brown as? (Leather)

Round as? (Ball)
Cold as? (Ice)
Hot as? (Fire, Sun)

CITIES AND COUNTRIES

The players are divided into two groups. The leader calls out the name of a city or country. Anyone in either group calls out what that place is noted for. Leader calls:

Paris (Eiffel Tower)
Spain (Bullfight)
London (Big Ben)
Egypt (Pyramids)
Ceylon (Tea)
India (Taj Mahal)
Norway (Fjords)
United States (Statue of Liberty)

MEMORY LANE

This game may be played when all the guests live in the same area of a town. The host indicates a specific block in the neighborhood. Guests are given paper and pencil. The purpose of the game is to list the names of homeowners and buildings in the block. The winner is the one with the most correct names and buildings.

MATCH BALANCE

Materials are a box of wooden matches and a bottle with a narrow neck (a pop bottle). The stunt is to see who can pile the most matches on top of the bottle. The matches are counted when the final match causes the others to fall.

Gossip

Players sit in a circle. One begins by whispering, once, a statement to the player on his right. Each player in turn whispers the statement, as he interprets it, to the person on his right. The last person tells aloud what he heard. The final statement will usually be entirely unlike the original statement.

8
FAMILY TRAVELS

Trips to visit relatives, places of interest, and vacation spots are often made by auto. How can the trip itself, with the family confined inside a car, be made an enjoyable experience? Draw children, mother, and father into the planning from the start, and give consideration to everyone's idea about the trip. With maps before the family, lay out your route. The shortest route is not always the most interesting one, if you are concerned about making the trip enjoyable and educational. If you are traveling across several states, agree on various responsibilities. One responsibility might be the job of looking up the geography of these states, the principle agricultural products and industry, and especially the size of the larger cities.

Taking unhurried time for the trip will add to the enjoyment and avoid the tension that comes from being rushed. Developing a time schedule that will permit stopping to visit places of interest, to take pictures, and to purchase postcards is a good idea.

Games to Play While Traveling

ANIMALS

Divide the members of the car into two teams, each team looking for animals on its side of the road. Rate animals of different kinds with different values; e.g., horses count 5, cows 3, hogs 2, and sheep 1. But a white horse gets an extra 8 points and a skunk, gopher, fox, or any unusual animal 10 points.

INSIDE THE CAR

Each member of the family in turn says, "I have something in mind which is . . ." and then gives the color of the object. The other members of the family attempt to guess what it is, and the number of guesses taken to locate the object is the score given to the person who had the object in mind.

GAS STATIONS

Each member of the family takes one of the popular gas company names. Score one point for each gas station passed for the person assigned to that particular company.

SCRAMBLE WORDS

Play with two or three persons. The words chosen should be taken from billboards en route. One person has a word in mind. He then spells out the chosen word by scrambling the letters. If the word is too difficult, the leader gives the first letter of the word. The first one to unscramble the word scores one point.

Signboard Alphabet

Again the family is divided into two groups, each one finding the letters of the alphabet on his side of the road. Each group attempts to go through the alphabet starting with "A" and continuing in order by locating these letters on mailboxes and billboards. Each group must see the other's letter to have it count. The first one to get through the entire alphabet wins the game.

Name the Car

Each of the members of the family chooses a familiar make of car, for example, Ford, Chevrolet, or Rambler. In a definite period of time, each one looks for the cars of his choice. One point is given for each car.

What Is It?

Mother or daddy holds up something gathered along the way. What is it? The family guesses.

Listen and Guess

Stop talking for three minutes. Everybody listens and reports on the sounds he hears.

I See

One member of the family says, "I see," and the others try to find the thing that he sees.

OBSERVING

Make a list of the various farm animals, signs, birds, trees, and pets that are seen during a thirty-minute period.

FIFTY MILES' SEARCH

A search for the most interesting or the most unusual thing within the next fifty miles. Each member of the family records what he believes to be the most unusual.

MOM'S OR DAD'S SECRETARY

Give the youngster (eight years or older) a notebook and pencil to keep a log of the entire trip. It can include the mileage readings at the beginning and the end of the day, the number of miles covered each hour, the amount of gas and oil consumed, the cost of fuel, and other expenditures for the car and passengers.

NAVIGATOR

An older child can be the navigator for the family. He will help with the itinerary of the trip and the selection of the route to follow. He can list all route numbers and all towns and cities in his notebook, checking them off one by one as you drive along. He can also keep an eye on the map and avoid wrong turns.

MEMORIES

Recall the different events of last years' trip. Note the people you met, the cities in which you stopped, the historical places, and the most unusual and most interesting part of the trip.

RELATIVES AND FRIENDS

If the visiting of friends and relatives is part of a trip, conversation about them can be interesting. Mother or dad should name the persons to be visited, and one of the older children should write the names of each and something about each person.

Note: It should be understood by the family that games of this kind ought to be interrupted when something of special interest comes into view. Also that whenever possible, permit the family to be creative and to make changes in the games, adding new enthusiasm with each change. If each game is played for only a short while, the family will be ready to play it again the following day. Do not continue to play the game when the interest begins to lag.

9

RAINY DAY ACTIVITIES

When weather conditions eliminate the great out-of-doors as a playground, it need not be tragedy for the family that has planned for such days. A rainy day can be an *opportunity* instead of a *calamity*. This can be the time for explorations into the attic, the basement, or other rooms where things have been put away because the out-of-doors has been more inviting.

There must be a willingness on the part of all members of the family to permit activities in some room, with permission to roll up carpets and rearrange furniture, making room for creative play with members of the family, neighbors, and friends. This is particularly helpful where a basement or a rumpus room is not available.

Individual Skill Tests

STANDING HIGH JUMP

Mark on the door frame a spot fifteen inches higher than you can reach when standing with arm raised. Now jump and see if you can reach the spot you have marked.

Sit Down

With one leg stretched out in front, lower your body to sit on your heel and then come to a stand.

Push-ups

Lie flat on the floor, face down and hands under chest. Raise your body off the floor until arms are straight, and lower body again, five times.

Push Away

Stand two feet away from a wall. Lean forward until your hands and chest are on the wall. Now push yourself back to a standing position without moving your feet.

Chalk Walk

Walk six feet on a line, heel to toe.

Jumping Jacks

Jump and click your feet together once, landing with feet apart. Then click feet together twice.

Stork Stand

Stand on one foot with the other foot on the inside of the knee.

Jump Through

Holding the right toe with the left hand, jump on the left foot.

Three-Quarter Pirouette

Jump in the air and land on both feet after making a three-quarter turn.

Full Pirouette

Jump in the air and land on both feet after making a full turn.

Frog Stand

A squat position, hands on floor inside of knees. Balance entire body on hands, lifting both feet off the floor.

Inside-Outside

Hands inside of knees, out and around legs to touch fingers in front of the body.

Other Activities

Tracing Pictures

An old magazine, a sheet of carbon paper, and a sheet of plain paper can keep a child entertained a long time in tracing the pictures onto the paper underneath.

Making a Drum

The very young may enjoy beating on the bottom of a box or on a piece of old inner tube stretched across the open end of a box and tied securely.

Bird Feeding Station

Place outside the child's window. Whether sick or not, he will enjoy watching the birds eat.

Sandbox Table

Nail retaining boards around a low table and put sand on it. This can be used in the basement or on the porch for bad days.

Decorated Paper Plates

Paste rickrack or paper doilies around the edge, draw pictures with crayon or tempera.

Trapeze

Fasten a trapeze to the basement ceiling joists. Small children will enjoy swinging on it.

Tenpins

Hang a ball on a string from the top of a door, and arrange bottles like tenpins below. Walk backwards, taking ball, and let it swing forward to knock down pins.

Book Repair

For rainy days, gather up the books that need to be mended, and all your mending material, and let the children help mend books.

Somersaults

If you have an old mattress, let the children use it for somersaults in the basement.

Picture Puzzles

A quick way to make a picture puzzle for a young child is to cut a picture postcard into four or five pieces. The card is stiff enough so that it need not be mounted. If the child can read, write a message on the back of the card before cutting. Thus the child will have two puzzles.

Rainy Day Games

Dot and Line

Draw a square consisting of lines of dots drawn horizontally and vertically. The two players take turns drawing horizontal and vertical lines to connect any two dots. The object of the game is to complete a square and to prevent an opponent from completing a square. Each time a player succeeds in drawing the fourth line of a square he puts his initials in it and draws another line. The one completing the most squares wins.

Battleship

Each person rules off two squares, with each square marked off into 100 small squares. On the top mark squares from A to J; on the left side of the large square mark each small square from 1 to 10. Each person locates

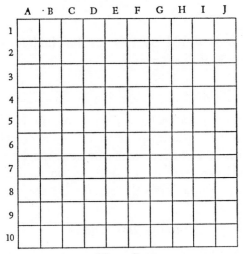

Your Ocean

in the upper square (now known as his ocean) four boats: a battleship, a cruiser, and two destroyers. The battleship covers four squares, the cruiser three, and each destroyer two squares. These may be put in vertically or horizontally. Your opponent must not know where you locate them. Now you are ready to play. Each in turn gets seven shots trying to locate and sink his opponent's ship.

You do this by calling a letter and a number to indicate the square; i.e., "B-4." Keep track of your own shots in the lower square. After each volley of seven shots, you tell your opponent if any of his shots hit any one of your ships. A boat is sunk when all the squares in which it lies have been hit. When a battleship is sunk, the owner has his total of seven shots reduced by three, for

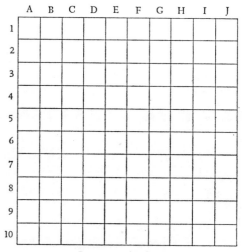

Opponent's Ocean

a cruiser two shots, and for each destroyer one shot. The first one to sink all of the opponent's ships wins.

Move a Mark

Place 12 marks in 3 rows on a piece of paper. In the first row put 5, in the second row 4, in the third row 3. Two players take turns crossing out marks. Each player in turn may cross out as many marks as he wishes from one row. On the first turn, therefore, a player may cross out from 1 to 5 marks.

Regardless of how many marks are removed, each player may cross out marks from only one row when it's his turn. The winner is the one who crosses out the last mark on the page.

10
FUN WHILE CONVALESCING

Being confined to bed during or following an illness need not be a period of complete idleness. Most doctors will recommend some kind of activity to speed up the return to normalcy.

Mental activities and simple writing games and stunts can be played with pencil and paper. A writing board (a plywood board shaped to fit around the patient) may serve as a desk when the individual is permitted to sit up in bed.

The nurse, mother, brother, sister, or friend who can stimulate some activity for the convalescent will add to the pleasure of a visit and will provide activity for the patient when he or she is alone.

FINGER GAMES

For the younger child, the use of hands and fingers in the making of various things can be a new experience.

A ball—Finger tips touching with hands cupped.

Child's hammer—One fist pounding the other.

Music—Hand clapping.

Soldiers—Ten fingers pointing upward.

Trumpet—Blowing through fists.
In jail—All fingers over eyes.
Baby's cradle—Clasp hands and rock-a-bye.

SHADOWGRAPHS

With a bed lamp behind the patient, the hands and fingers may be manipulated in ways that the shadow cast on the wall will resemble the heads of various animals, such as a dog, rabbit, camel, bear, wolf, goat, or an elephant.

EXPLORE THE ROOM

With older children, having them explore with imagination the various aspects of the room to which they are confined can be interesting. This could be done by first guessing the dimensions of the room, the weight of various objects such as books, lamps, or the age of other equipment being used.

MOTOR COORDINATION

Motor coordination can be practiced and perfected while convalescing. Here are a few exercises that can be done while reclining or sitting up:

1. Circle the chin with a finger of one hand while you rub the nose up and down with the other.

2. Tap head several times with one hand while you rub the stomach in circular motion with the other hand.

3. Make a small circle clockwise with left hand while you make a circle in the opposite direction with the other.

4. Hold your nose with left hand while you hold left ear with the right hand. On the count of three, clap your hands and change the positions of your hands. (The right hand to your nose and your left hand to your right ear.)

Crossed Match Trick (for one player)

Take two wooden matches. Cross them with the right-hand one on top, then hold them with the thumb and first finger of the right hand without touching the ends or the place where they are crossed.

Card and Coin Trick (for one player)

Place a small thin card on the end of the left middle finger. On that place a small coin, for example, a dime. Then with the right thumb and first or second finger, snap the card out, leaving the coin on the end of the finger.

Scissors Trick (for one player)

Hold your hands out in front of you with the palms up and the little fingers side by side. Take a pair of blunt scissors and hang them with the points down on the little fingers, one finger through each handle. Now throw the scissors over so that they lie on the hands with the points toward you. Do not release the hold with the little fingers. Turn the scissors between your arms, and turn the hands so that the backs are together and the scissors are open, with the points up.

The trick is done by keeping the scissors closed and the fists close together until the last move brings the backs of the hands together and opens the scissors. The little fingers are not taken out of the rings in the handle of the scissors while the trick is being done.

THIRTEEN PUZZLE (for two players)

Place thirteen objects on a table. Each player in turn may take one, two, or three at a time. The aim is to make one's opponent take the last one.

THE SURPRISE BOX

A special box, made out of an old shoe box, is placed in the front hall for the convalescent. The family keeps the box supplied with letters and little gifts, wrapped up in gay packages. The child goes to his box every morning for his surprise.

COOKING

Boys as well as girls like to have a hand in cooking and baking along with mother. There are several cookbooks and recipes that can be followed by children when they learn to read.

HAND PUPPETS

You can make a puppet by just using your fist. Take a napkin or handkerchief and tie it on your fist for a hat. Draw a face on the back of your hand.

My Father Keeps a Grocery Store (for two or more players)

A player says, "My father keeps a grocery store. He keeps 'p' (pickles)." The others guess what "p" stands for, and whoever guesses correctly is next to keep the grocery store. They do not guess in turn, but whenever they choose to do so.

Train

Make a train of chairs in a line, with conductor, caboose, passengers. The ingenuity of children usually supplies the rest, such as whistle, bell, lights, motion.

Treasure Hunt

An indoor treasure hunt is fun. Clues are placed all over the house for children to find. Sometimes the note may say, "Sing a song here," or "Play a certain game here," "Cut out pictures," etc., even with treats here and there, and a grand treasure at the end of the line.

Vegetable Puppets

You can make puppets with vegetables, too. Any vegetables shaped like potatoes, turnips, etc., can be used for puppet heads. Cut faces in the skin or paint them on.

Ticktacktoe (for two players)

A diagram is drawn on a board or table. Each player is given five checkers. One has red and the other black.

They take turns placing their checkers, one at a time, on the board in the spaces. The one who succeeds in getting three in a row wins the game. The rows may be horizontal, vertical, or diagonal. See chapter 6 for variation.

A Sick Box

During the time when the children are well, accumulate things they will enjoy when they are sick. Here are some suggestions:

1. Paper, pencils, crayons, scissors, scraps of cloth, needles, buttons.
2. Coloring books or things to color.
3. Simple craft projects.
4. Old magazines for cutting paper dolls, making a scrapbook of dogs, cats, people.
5. Sewing kits, dolls to dress.
6. Materials for making puppets or flowers.
7. A special, gay tray for the bed.
8. Surprises, like balloons, bubble gum.

Growing Plants

Watching the progress of gardens grown from grapefruit or orange pits, radish or pumpkin seeds, gives a youngster something to look forward to each day. Soak the seeds overnight before planting them. Then cover them with ¼ inch of soil.

A sweet potato partly immersed in water will sprout a leafy vine. If you put it in a glass jar, you can watch the roots grow, as well as the buds. A piece of an ordinary

101

white potato with two or three eyes will grow if planted about three inches deep in a flower pot.

DRAWING

Large sheets of paper are best suited for children's use. The youngest children like to scribble with big fat crayons of all colors. A small blackboard or slate provides endless amusements, because drawings are so easily erased.

CATALOGS

For the boy or girl confined to the four walls of a bedroom, the pages of a mail-order catalog are magic peepholes to the outside world. A girl can pretend that she is furnishing a new house. A boy may choose to equip a farm, selecting machinery, tools, and the seeds he must order.

WEATHER OBSERVATION

A child might observe the weather every day for a month. Draw a yellow sun, a black cloud, or a gay umbrella, to indicate what happens each day. Record the temperature. Keep a scorecard when listening to the weather reports to find out how accurate his predictions are.

11
FAMILY CRAFTS

To make a thing of beauty or usefulness with one's own hands is recreation of a special sort. There is within all of us the ability to create beauty if we honestly try. There are countless simple handcrafts that all of us can make to beautify our homes or adorn ourselves, or that can be used for quick, satisfying recreation.

This chapter deals with crafts which can be developed with simple equipment and with materials frequently discarded or available from a garden, in the fields, or along the roadside.

The following suggestions for the selection of materials, the use of simple equipment, and the directions for making should make it easy for anyone to participate in a good craft program.

Plastic Bottles

Many bleaches, starches, soaps, etc., now come in plastic bottles that can easily be cut with sturdy scissors. Simple planters can be made by cutting the top off a bottle. Slits cut down the sides can be curled around a pencil. Cover with rope or crepe paper to make a hanging flower container.

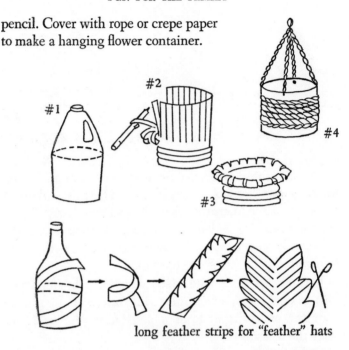

long feather strips for "feather" hats

Long feather strips cut from plastic can be used for many decorative purposes. Combine this technique with the above ideas for more creative projects. Save all the scraps for making jewelry.

JEWELRY FROM DISCARDED ARTICLES

Saw an old broom handle into discs—decorate and drill holes through center for dress buttons. Several coats of shellac or varnish will make them waterproof.

Corncob sawed into discs—use rug yarn to string on for an interesting necklace.

Shelled corn sewn through the small end in long single strands—twist several strands together to make a showy necklace.

Macaroni and spaghetti jewelry—cooked and shaped while still wet (put the shaped wet object on a piece of paper toweling so it won't "crawl" while drying). When dry, nail polish will give it a bright finish. Glue it to earring backs, pin backs, etc.

An old toothbrush handle makes a ring—measure finger, cut exact length from handle. Drop in boiling water. Shape with pliers while hot. File or sand a design on.

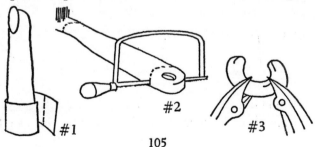

#1   #2   #3

105

Earring backs and pin backs of all types are found in most department stores at very reasonable prices.

Cover pretty stones (garden variety) with a coat of clear nail polish to make them shine. Wrap with thin wire to form a loop to hang them with.

TIN CAN CRAFTING

The tools needed are very simple. Tin snips or an old pair of scissors, hammer, a wall-type can opener, a nail for tapping designs, and perhaps solder (liquid solder requires no soldering iron). The tin cans are easily acquired. Check for interesting colors and textures—the inside of various cans are quite colorful and many cans have decorative stripes running around them. Don't throw any part of the can away—it is all useful. To cut a can easily, remove the top rim by inserting the open end in a wall-type can opener sideways. Reverse ends and cut the bottom off the same way. You now have a cylindrical shape—cut the seam out with the tin snips or an old pair of scissors.

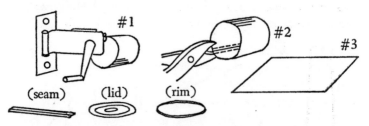

(seam) (lid) (rim)

Roll side out flat. You now have 2 rims, 2 lids, a seam, and a big sheet of metal to work with. The rim can be used for Christmas tree decorations, the lid can be hammered into a bowl, and the seam saved for reinforcing. Your objects can be painted, hammered, modeled, tooled, etched, shaped; and a simple way to put a design on them is with hammer and nail. Sketch design with pencil, put metal on a stack of newspapers, outline design and fill in areas by indenting—a blow of the hammer on the nail head. Cut strips in the metal and shape with pliers for interesting scroll work.

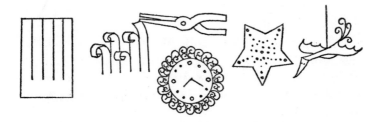

Imitation Leather from Inner Tubes

Discarded inner tubes offer a variety of textures— rough, designed—and either side of them can be used. Inner tubing can be used for all things leather is used for except for tooling or stamping. It can be carved or have a design punched in, or the design could be cut out and rubber-cemented to the article. Stuffed toys, pocketbooks and beach bags, billfolds, belts, beanies, moccasins, notebook covers are some of the things that can be made from inner tubes. Punch holes with a leather punch and lace with shoestrings, heavy twine, or long strips of inner tubing. Use rubber cement for attaching pieces.

CREPE PAPER RAFFIA

Cut a one-inch strip off the end (cross grain) of an entire roll of crepe paper. Tie end of strip through a

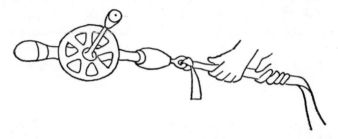

screw eye inserted in a hand drill. One person stretches the strip as the other person turns the drill. One package of crepe paper 20 inches x 10 feet will make 20 strips of raffia, each strip about 18 inches long—enough for several projects.

This raffia can be knitted, crocheted, wrapped, glued to objects, inlayed, or used as tie string for gift wrapping. Variations include:

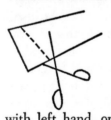

Cut strips from ½ inch to 1½ inches wide for assorted sizes.

Cut one strip diagonally for size variation.

Combine two colors before twisting to make variegated raffia (stretch one with left hand, one with right hand, as drill is turned).

Twist together two colored strips that have already been twisted for raffia.

Braid the twisted raffia.

Some of the things that can be made from crepe paper raffia are covered bottles, jugs, flowerpots, hot mats, vases, flowers, animals, lampshades, dolls, boxes, coasters, baskets, purses, wastebaskets, book-ends, picture frames, book covers, table mats.

Mosaics

There are endless possibilities for mosaic design. Mosaics can be used for design on wood, plywood, cardboard, metal, glass, cement, paper, etc. They can range in size from the smallest area to a large wall picture—mural size. The range of material for mosaics includes scrap ceramic tile, linoleum, the garden variety of stones, breakfast foods, macaroni, spaghetti, noodles, plastic from bottles, seeds of all kinds, beads, old crayons, crushed glass and pottery, confetti, paper, felt from old hats, sawdust, coffee grounds, oyster shells, sea shells, eggshells.

First sketch your design on your background. Glue the pieces of material in place on top of the sketch. If you

109

are using thin materials such as paper, put the pieces apart a bit so there is an area left between each piece. If you are using heavy material such as tile, when the glue is dry, work a coat of plaster of paris into all the cracks. Wait fifteen minutes and remove the excess with a damp cloth. Allow to dry.

The results are spectacular! This is a very good way of renewing old furniture such as table tops, trays, etc. Try it around wastebaskets and planters. Discarded cans can be made into useful items by applying mosaic.

Papier-Mâché

Anything from giant outdoor decorations to dainty jewelry can be made from papier-mâché. It is very suitable for puppet heads, relief maps, sculpture, vases, chessmen, dishes, toys, serving trays, candle holders, etc.

Chicken wire, wire coat hangers, cardboard tubes, or rolled or crushed newspapers, can be used as a skeletal frame on which to build the mâché object. Paper for making mâché includes newspaper, magazines, wrapping

base

paper, toweling, toilet paper, napkins, confetti, feed bags, packing paper, shredded paper, or any absorbant paper.

Any water-soluable paste may be used. The simplest paste is 1½ cups water and 1 cup flour (not self-rising). Hints: (1) Be generous with the paste; (2) always tear the paper (smoother appearance); (3) alternate layers of plain newspaper and colored comic sections so you know how many layers you have put on.

Layered mâché is a sandwich made of several sheets (full size) of newspaper with a filling of paste between each layer. This drapes and shapes well over wire.

Torn strips work on large or medium-sized objects; hand-sized pieces on medium or small objects; very small pieces, shredded paper, or confetti work well for small objects.

Dried objects can be sanded, sawed, or cut with knife or razor blade. Then they may be painted with any type of paint, shellacked, or varnished for a waterproof surface.

Modeling Mâché

Many types of mâché or clay-like mixtures can be used for modeling. One of the simplest is sawdust mâché, which is easily workable, dries in about 48 hours, is very sturdy, sands easily, and takes paint well. To 1½ cups of water add 1 cup flour (not self-rising) and 3 cups of sawdust. Mix with hands. Small objects can be formed easily. Larger objects will dry more rapidly if they are built around a cardboard tube or crushed newspaper.

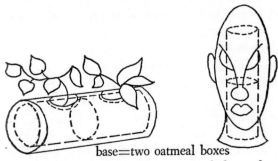

base=two oatmeal boxes

The flour-water paste makes a good base for wood shavings, excelsior, cloth, vermiculite, or any absorbant scraps. The lint saver in the clothes dryer is a good source of filler for mâché.

Any mâché should be air-dried. If dried rapidly, it will develop cracks. If cracks do develop, fill with more mixture and dry again.

When dry, paint. Shellac or varnish, several coats, for a waterproof finish.

The flour-water paste is a good base for absorbant string, yarn, rope, etc., to make airy mobiles. These materials also make delightful Easter eggs. Blow up a balloon and tie knot in the neck. Dip the yarn in the paste mixture and carefully drape or wind it around the balloon. Hang to dry. When dry, puncture balloon and remove.

Corn Husk Dolls

Save the husks of field corn—dry. Outer husks of sweet corn may be used. Those dried outdoors may be used, or if dried indoors, they will retain their soft green color. If husks are badly stained, bleach them. If you desire color, dye them, rinse in cold water, and dry.

When ready to start on the doll, soak the husks in warm water for about five minutes to make them pliable. Work with damp husks. These damp husks will shape well and will work up easily.

Use small strips of husks for attaching and holding in shape.

Sand Painting

You will need nice clean silica sand and tempera colors. One cup sand to ½ teaspoon color—stir with spoon until sand is evenly coated. Spread on newspaper to dry, stirring frequently. When completely dry, sand may be stored in covered containers. Paint with the colored sand on paper or cardboard by first sketching your picture. Paint the area to be colored one color with clear mucilage. While it is moist, sprinkle the colored sand over it and allow a second or two for it to dry. Shake off excess (back into container) and paint another area for your second color. Continue until all areas are colored. When completely dry, the work may be sprayed with a clear spray to seal from dust.

CHRISTMAS TREE DECORATIONS

Accumulate such throw-away items as foil dishes, used flash bulbs, bottle caps and toothpaste caps, burnt matches, toothpicks, drinking straws, sucker and ice cream sticks, egg cartons, plastic bottles, discarded jewelry, scraps of cotton, felt, and dress materials, etc. Have glue and paint or fingernail polish, some string and wire, scissors (old pinking shears are very useful) and glitter ready to use with your throw-away items. It's fun to combine these items into unusual tree decorations.

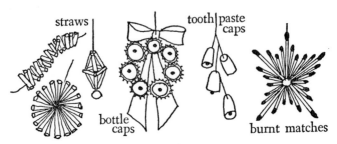

straws | tooth|paste caps

bottle caps

burnt matches

12
BACKYARD ACTIVITIES

Family fun in the out-of-doors, particularly in your own yard, can be a source of real family enjoyment. Planning the kind of equipment, activities, and the placing of trees and garden should be a family project. Lighting up a yard play area should add much time for the use of the backyard. Beautifying the yard as well as purchasing or making equipment can be a family project. The following pieces of equipment can be a real asset in making the most of the yard: a picnic table, outdoor grill, basketball goal, badminton court, sandbox, tent, and a sled for winter use.

The following equipment can easily be obtained or made at home:

1. Planks of wood, 12 inches wide by 8 feet long, slightly elevated from the ground, which can become a hill for trucks and cars.
2. Empty crates and boxes.
3. Old tires to roll or crawl through.
4. Blocks for construction 4 inches by 10 inches by 10 inches.

5. A strong rope hung from a tree for climbing or swinging.
6. Beanbags.

The driveway, often overlooked as a part of yard play area, makes an excellent area on which to paint shuffleboard, cut-the-pie, or variations of Sky Blue and hopscotch.

Games for the Backyard

CROQUET

A good game for both family and visitors.

GARDEN GOLF

Use rubber ball, broom handle for a club, and pegs instead of holes.

BOCCIE BALL

An Italian game which can be modified to suit conditions, using soft balls or tennis balls, four balls to a team. The game can be played by two or four, either singly or in teams. The game is started by throwing a smaller colored ball any distance, long or short depending on the yard. The teams take turns throwing their balls to the target ball. The individual or side wins whose ball or balls are closest to the target. One point is given for each ball closest to the target. The side winning the last point then tosses the target ball to a new position, near or far, and the game resumes. Twenty-one points is a game.

116

Rubber Quoits

See chapter 2.

Marble Golf

In this novel game, of which there are a number of variations, a nine-hole course is laid out around the yard. Small tin cans are sunk in the ground. Four players start off and shoot marbles, counting the shots taken to get the marbles into the cans. Hazards may be small bushes, lengths of four-inch pipe through which the golfer must shoot, little troughs, and boards with four-inch holes through which the marbles must go.

Swing

Every yard must have a swing. If there is no tree, you can, of course, have a wooden frame for your swing.

Teeter-Totter

Preschool children soon discover that a sawhorse plus a sturdy plank of spruce or other long-grained wood equals a teeter-totter. Be sure that the sawhorse is low enough for safety.

The plank may also be used as a bridge, a slide, a gangplank, or as an incline at various heights for running and jumping off. Raised from the ground on boxes or low saw horses, a plank helps children gain self-confidence and balance and provides thrilling springboard action. The plank also can make a fine balancing beam.

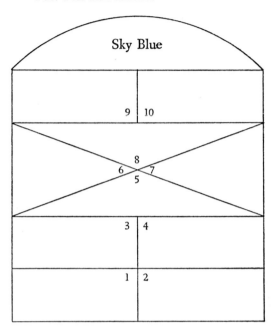

SKY BLUE

Each player in turn tosses a marker in the No. 1 square, hops in on one foot, retrieves marker, hops out. He continues tossing marker into successive squares, hopping into each one and out as long as he tosses marker successfully and does not step on any lines. The game continues through the "sky blue" area at end, then back to "start" in reverse order.

HOPSCOTCH

Each player in turn tosses marker into each successive square, retrieves it by hopping on one foot. He continues his turn until he steps on a line or fails to toss marker into correct square. The first one to reach the "finish" square can put his initials into any square, which others

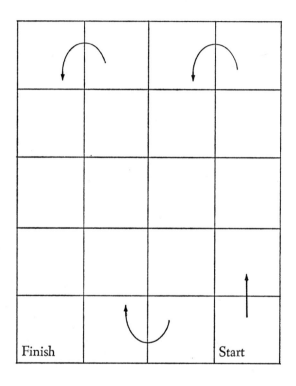

Finish

Start

must then jump over. As others finish, they add their initials to a square which then becomes a "rest" square to "owner" and an obstacle to be jumped over by the others. The game continues thus until all squares are initialed.

A Horizontal Bar

A horizontal bar may be made of two uprights, 6 inches by 6 inches by 10 feet; four braces, 4 inches by 4 inches by 6 feet; and a piece of galvanized pipe, 1¼ inches by 6 feet.

Duck

"It" tries to tag a player. The only way to avoid being tagged is to squat like a duck. A person tagged while standing or falling becomes "It." Players must take five steps before they squat, then rise, and take five more steps before they squat again; or leader says, "Up, down, move" at intervals.

Ear and Foot

"It" can tag anyone who does not hold his ear with one hand and his foot with other hand while resting. Players can run as they please to evade "It."

Pose

Group decides on a pose—such as an animal, the Statue of Liberty, an angel. Players cannot be tagged by "It" when they assume the pose. If they leave their pose they must move ten paces before assuming a new pose. They can be tagged while moving.

Cross Tag

"It" may chase anyone and must tag him before another player crosses him out—that is, runs between "It" and his quarry. The player who intervened becomes the new quarry. If tagged, he becomes "It."

OBJECT TAG

The group runs about freely in a small designated area. One player has the object. Another player is "It" and tries to tag the holder of the object. Players pass (not toss) the object to one another as they try to avoid being tagged while carrying it.

LEAPFROG TAG

All players except two squat in frog position. Standing player No. 1 chases standing player 2. No. 2 may leapfrog over any squating player. As soon as he does this, No. 2 squats to frog position and the player he leaped over must take his place in the tag game.

OSTRICH TAG

Person who is "It" can tag anyone who is not standing on one leg and holding the other leg with his hand.

WASHER PITCHING

Get a couple of dozen large metal washers from a hardware store. Draw a target with bull's eye 8 inches in diameter; the next circle 16 inches; and the outside one 24 inches. Three points for bull's eye, two points for the 16-inch circle, and one point for hitting in the outside circle. Players throw or slide washers into the target. Game is 21 points. Also use them like horseshoes. Outdoors, sink two large tin cans into the ground, arranged like a horseshoe court. Players toss washers into the cans. (Distance apart depends on age of players.)

BEANBAG TOSS

The beanbags have to go into the cans to score. Toss from position several feet back. Set a top limit for the game.

STONE'S THROW

Draw a target on the ground with several circles. Number the bull's eye the highest score. Two players have an even number of stones for markers. Object is to get highest score. An opponent's stone cancels your stone if it lands in the same circle. Stones can be of different colors or sizes or marked with chalk.

CORK TOSS

Get a bunch of corks of different sizes. Let players try to toss them into a box or can.

BOTTLE CAP TOSS

Players try to toss caps from soft drink bottles into a can, basket, or box.

13
FAMILY PICNICS

A family picnic can be worth the effort. It should not be an event where mother does all the work. It should be a family event where all the members share in the work, including shopping, preparing the food, selecting the place to go and the activities of the day.

Games and fun are a part of picnics. To take along a ball, horseshoes, metal washers for pitching, or even reading material, means that the family is better prepared to have a good time. It is fun to take advantage of the nature setting, in which picnics are usually held, with nature games.

What to take along on a picnic: Plates, cups, knives, forks, teaspoons, tablespoons, large knife for cutting, can opener, bottle opener, containers for salt, pepper, sugar, butter, salad dressing, cocoa. (Paper utensils can be burned.) If the meal is to be prepared partially or entirely out of doors, add a pail or pot for beverages, covered kettle, frying pan, long-handled spoon and fork, matches, soap, and hand towels. Other helpful equipment would be a wire broiler, folding grate, reflectors, pot holder, camp stove.

Good desserts are fruits, fruit salad, cookies, cupcakes, doughnuts, crackers and cheese. S'mores are good—toasted marshmallows in the gooey stage placed between flat pieces of sweetened chocolate in graham cracker sandwiches. Rice pudding with raisins, butter, and sugar is also popular.

Delegate a share in the responsibilities of unpacking, fire building, table setting, cooking, and cleaning up to each member of the picnic party.

Cooking Outdoors

Besides just roasting wieners or frying hamburgers, there are many things your family can do out of doors, cooking its own food.

Cheese bobs: Securely wrap a piece of cheese about an inch square in a piece of bacon, pierce with stick, and broil over hot coals. Drop finished product on buttered roll.

Banana bobs: Cut a peeled banana in half crosswise, wrap in a thin slice of bacon or dried beef, skewer on a stick, and broil over the coals. Eat in a toasted buttered bun.

Doghouse biscuits: Make biscuit dough of prepared biscuit flour and shape it by hand in a thin layer over Vienna sausages or small frankfurters. Toast slowly over fire, allowing 10 minutes to bake the biscuit dough.

Little pig potatoes: With a coring knife, remove from one end the centers of medium-sized Irish or sweet potatoes, just enough to make room for small sausages; stuff, close with piece of potato core. Scrape hot coals aside, lay potato in hot earth or sand and cover with same, piling coals on top. (The potatoes could be wrapped in wet leaves, wet brown paper, or mud. If encased in mud, put in direct contact with coals.) Allow 45—60 minutes for baking.

Bacon, cheese, or raw egg also make tasty stuffing for Irish potatoes. If an egg is used, keep the potato upright. Brown sugar, raisins, and marshmallows may be used in sweet potatoes in place of sausages.

Pit apples: Remove core without having hole all the way through, stuff with raisins and brown sugar, marshmallows, or sausage. Allow 30—45 minutes for baking, depending on the coals.

Roasting corn: Soak ears of corn in bucket of salt water 10 minutes, hang corn over coals and allow to cook 30 minutes. (Inspect for worms before cooking, but do not remove shucks.)

Kabobs: Cut bacon and steak into small pieces, 1½ inches square. Slice onions in quarters from stem part down. Place on sharpened and peeled stick of sweet wood 3/4 inch thick or less, alternating the bacon, steak, and onion slices, but leaving a little space between each piece. Broil over hot coals until well done. Place between slices of buttered bread or between halves of a roll. Other vegetables may be added.

Roasted apple: Char the end of a sharpened green stick, plunge it into cold water. Spike an apple, roast until skin peels off easily. Roll apple in brown sugar. Hold it over coals and turn slowly until the sugar candies.

Races

ROLLING RACE

All lie down straight, a few feet separating each, and roll to the finish line, hands over heads.

DISCUS THROW

Use paper plates.

DUCK RACE

Stoop and grasp ankles with hands, and waddle along to the finish line.

BALLOON RACE

Each child has a balloon to bat along to the finish line.

BACK-TO-BACK RACE

For this contest, contestants go in pairs back to back with elbows linked.

BOX RACE

The players have their feet in two cartons and advance by sliding them along in running or walking motions. Only two cartons are allowed per team, so each contestant must change when he returns to the starting line.

SORE TOE RACE OR RELAY

Each contestant must hold his foot either in front of him or behind him and hop to the finish line. If this is used as a relay, at the turning line have him grasp his other foot and hop back on the opposite foot.

Other Events

Hot Hand

A player, kneeling down, places his face, eyes closed, in the lap of another. He places his hand on his back, palm up. Each person walks up and slaps the open hand. After each slap the kneeler tries to guess who hit him. If he guesses correctly, that player takes his place.

Variation: Instead of kneeling, the player may bend over with his head against his arm, resting against a tree or wall.

Loose Caboose

Form trains by having players line up in groups of three, one behind the other, holding one another around the waist or arms. The first in line is the "engine," the next the "coal car," and the last the "caboose." One or more players are the "loose cabooses." They try to catch on to the end of the various trains. When a caboose is successful, the "engine" of the group goes off to become the loose caboose.

Keep-up

Divide group into small teams and give each two teams a balloon. The balloon is tossed into the air and each team swats the balloon alternately trying to keep it in the air. The team that misses it before it touches the ground loses a point.

Blues and Blacks

Two equal lines face each other, close enough together to be able to shake hands. Each side has a goal line back 10 feet or more. One side represents the "Blues" and the other the "Blacks." When the leader calls, "Blues," the "Blacks" try to catch them before they get back to the goal line. If caught, they must go to the other side. When "Blacks" are called, the "Blues" try to catch them. The side having more players in the time allotted for the game wins.

Act Out a Joke

Each person thinks of a joke and acts it out.

Clap-Out Rhythm

Each person thinks of a tune and claps out the rhythm of it for the others to guess.

Nail Driving Contest

Divide into groups and see which group can drive a nail straight through an old piece of 2 by 4 inch wood in the fewest strokes. Each member must hit in rotation. In other words, daddy can't do it all. (See also the home-made games in this book for other suggestions of simple games of skill to use with families in groups.)

HAND AND FIST

Everyone is asked to close the left hand with knuckles pointing down. Open the right hand, palm up. Insert the little finger of the right hand into the left-hand fist. Now in a four-count rhythm, reverse the position of hands four times. Repeat several times. Variation: Repeat above four counts, then continue for four counts turning the open hand over with palm down each time, with thumb going into fist.

SWEETHEARTS

Form a tent with fingers and thumbs of both hands touching. Keep fingers pointed upward while the two middle fingers point downward up to the second knuckle. Keeping the middle fingers together *all* the time, separate little fingers (brothers), then thumbs (sisters), then index fingers (friends). Now try to separate the ring finger next to the little finger. (These are sweethearts which cannot be separated.)

HAND SLAP

Players are in twos. One player extends both hands, palms down, and the other, both hands palms up and underneath hands of the other. The one whose hands are underneath quickly withdraws (or pretends to) his hands, slapping backs of hands of opponent, who tries to pull away his hands before they are slapped. If the underneath one succeeds, he or she continues as the hitter. If he fails, opponent gets opportunity.

Outdoor Bowling

Using a softball and pop bottles, set up as tenpins, follow the rules of regular bowling.

Shoe Kicking

With shoe loose on toe, each person kicks his shoe into the air and ahead of him as far as possible, hoping to be the winner.

Cane Catch

All the players but one stand in a circle. The one player in the center has a cane. He holds the cane straight up. Suddenly he calls the name of one in the circle and lets the cane go. The player so named must rush out and catch the cane before it reaches the floor. If the cane reaches the floor the victim changes places with "It."

Grab Ball

Players are numbered from one to the total number of players and formed into a circle. The leader from inside the circle tosses a ball into the air and calls a number. Player whose number is called must catch the ball or become the leader. If he catches the ball the leader remains "It." If he fails to grab it, he must do the number calling.

14
FAMILY WINTER FUN

Outdoor winter hobbies are as numerous as outdoor summer hobbies, and they are frequently the same hobbies that are popular in summer. A few are presented on the next pages. Most of them can be enjoyed by children and adults. Some of them can be carried on whether or not there is snow.

Winter Nature Hobbies

SNOWFLAKES

The simplest way to examine snowflakes is to catch them on the coat sleeve or let them fall on a dark cloth or paper. Teachers often place a dark cloth on the windowsill to catch flakes, which are then examined by the class through the windowpane, and their designs used as inspiration for cut-out work and art work. Snowflake cut-outs and designs can be used to decorate windows, hung from arches and doorways as mobiles, or used as Christmas ornaments.

There are probably billions of snowflakes formed in every snowfall, but no two are alike. Their only similarity is that each is a six-sided or six-pointed pattern. Basically there are three types of flakes most often seen: *stellar,* a starlike flake with six projecting ice crystals; *plate,* a six-sided flat flake; and *hexagonal plate,* with crystal extensions. Each snowflake is a collection of thousands of ice crystals.

FROST

In an area where there is no snow, frost observation can be a hobby. Frost is formed on the ground when the surface layer of air cools to the point where it loses some of its moisture. Frost on the windowpane is the result of low temperatures outside, cold enough to chill the inside air as it touches the window glass. Frost can be studied outdoors, in the early morning. The frost observer should crouch close to the ground and use a magnifying glass to see the delicate needle patterns.

WINTER HIKING

Hikes and picnics in wintertime give the nature collector or observer opportunity to look for treasures. He can sharpen his wits and test his observation by playing nature games. He can collect the stones or twigs or dried flowers or whatever it is he needs for his at-home nature projects.

On a family hike, collect a paper bag full of small nature objects, and use these for a blindfold identification game at the lunch stop or around a picnic fire or after reaching home. Objects should be put in the bag immediately when found, so they are not familiar to the entire group. Objects might be a stone, shell, twig, bird eggshell, bird feather, piece of bark, dried winter flower, vine tendril, hard fungus or lichen, animal bone or skeleton, plant gall.

ANIMAL TRACKS AND TRACKING

Snow-covered terrain provides wonderful opportunities to watch for and trail animals. The easiest way to start on a tracking hobby is to watch the cats, dogs, squirrels, and rabbits in the backyard or neighborhood.

BIRD TRACKING

Bird tracking is as much a hobby as animal tracking. Imprints of hopping birds and perching birds show paired tracks, such as those left by the hopping sparrow, blue jay, cardinal. The ground birds show alternated walking tracks, one foot placed ahead of the other, such as the starling, pheasant, bobwhite. The robin hops and walks.

WINTER FLOWER COLLECTIONS

Winter decorations, bouquets, and holiday decorations can be made from natural material found in winter woods and fields. Late fall and early winter are the best times to collect, when weeds and leaves are dry but not yet snow covered.

133

WINTER ASTRONOMY

The winter star show is often more brilliant than the summer star show. The clear, cold atmosphere emphasizes the glitter of the stars. Many of the most brilliant and noticeable star groups come into view only in the winter. The winter brilliance also depends on the distance of the star from the earth, the size of the star, and the temperature of the star.

A small telescope, or even powerful binoculars or field glasses, will be a help in star study. Star guidebooks and charts should be consulted.

FEEDING BIRDS

Many summer bird watchers carry their hobby over to the winter months and set up bird-feeding projects. Feeding of birds in winter is especially important in heavy snow-fall areas where much of the natural winter food is covered for weeks at a time.

Several feeding stations are needed if bird watching is to be a serious winter hobby. One station for suet, one for seed, one for grit, and one for drinking water. In addition, there should be a bathing station. All food should be convenient to perches.

WINTER PHOTOGRAPHY

Winter photography offers drama and contrast of light and dark in subjects that are impossible to snap in warm weather. Winter photography may numb your fingers, but the unusual pictures make it worthwhile.

WINTER RECORDS

Use a ruler or yardstick to measure depth of snow on different days. Keep a record of the depths and dates of snowfalls. Record the dates of the first snow, last snow, heaviest snowfall. Record daily temperatures during snow season. Measure icicles and see who finds the longest one.

Informal Snow Fun

Those who live where winter means snow and ice have an advantage. They can enjoy both the games and sports that require snow and ice and the games and sports that are generally familiar in areas where ice and snow are infrequently or never experienced.

Children, young people, families, small groups can have fun in the snow in many ways. Skiing and skating require skill, but anyone can have informal fun, such as that suggested here.

SNOW ANGELS

Find an area of undisturbed snow. Sit down, then lie flat on back with arms outstretched. Move arms toward head and then down to sides to make angel wings. Rise carefully to leave a neat impression. Angels are best made on a slope.

CUT-THE-PIE

On the new-fallen snow stamp a large circle. Then stamp several radii to the center like a sliced pie. This can then be the basis for a good game of tag.

House Floor Plans

Lay out a complete house floor plan in the snow. This can be actual dimension, with furniture made from snow and walls made of piled-up snow.

Snow Drawing

Draw pictures in the snow using feet only. Make designs, animals, trees, buildings, write messages, or lay a trail of symbols to lead to some treasure or hiding place.

Snow Sculpture

The first simple creation is formed from rolled balls of snow, placed on top of one another, with a crosspiece of wood or broomstick for arms. Characterization is added with stones, lumps of coal, old hats, sticks, toothpicks, colored glass.

This simple creation has developed into an elaborate technique of snow modeling and sculpture, used on playgrounds, in communities where winter decoration is encouraged, and in winter carnivals. From a roly-poly snowman made of three balls, the art of snow sculpture has turned to statues of people and animals; models of ships, airplanes, buildings, automobiles; copies in ice of famous paintings; landscapes; slogans worked out in ice and snow; characters from books or history.

Methods of making the snow and ice base: Every artist in ice and snow has his preferred method of building the base for his work. One way is to pile up a great block or mound of snow; let it freeze until it is a solid block of snow ice. This is then hacked and carved with an ax and hatchet.

Another method is to freeze blocks or cubes of solid ice and carve these into statues. Still another method is to build a wall of snow and freeze it by spraying water on it. This wall is then used for cutting a scene in high and low relief.

Snow Forts

Roll snowballs to a uniform size and stack them to form a wall or fort. Or form blocks from snow by packing snow in a box and tipping the blocks into place. Push a broomstick through the walls to make lookouts.

Snow or Ice Slides

Make a hill by piling up snow. Use it for sliding, rolling, tumbling downhill. Pour water over level snow to make a 2-foot-wide slide. Use it for running and sliding on feet, seat, or stomach.

For Further Reading

1. Family Recreation

Brightbill, Charles K. *Man and Leisure: A Philosophy of Recreation.* Englewood Cliffs, N. J.: Prentice-Hall, 1961.

Calkins, E. E. *The Care and Feeding of Hobby Horses.* New York: Sentinel Books, 1933.

Dulles, Foster R. *History of Recreation: America Learns to Play.* New York: (Appleton) Meredith, 1966.

Harbin, E. O. *Fun Encyclopedia.* Nashville: Abingdon Press, 1940.

2. Equipment and Games

Games for Quiet Hours and Small Spaces. New York: National Recreation and Park Association.

Homemade Play Apparatus. New York: National Recreation and Park Association.

Rohrbough, Lynn. *Handy II.* Delaware, Ohio: Cooperative Recreation Service, 1936.

What to Make for Children. New York: Popular Mechanics Press.

3. Fun at Mealtimes

Botkin, B. A. (ed.). *Treasury of American Folklore.* New York: Crown Publishers, 1944.

Folk Tales to Tell or Read Aloud. New York: National Recreation and Park Association.

Operation Family Fun. New York: National Recreation and Park Association.

4. Family Birthday Parties

Depew, Arthur M. *Cokesbury Party Book,* Rev. Ed. Nashville: Abingdon Press, 1959.

Musselman, Virginia. *Informal Dramatics.* New York: National Recreation and Park Association.

5. Holidays Together

Edgren, Harry D. *1,000 Games and Stunts.* Nashville: Abingdon Press, 1945.

Grove, Ernest R., *et al. The Family and Its Relationships.* Philadelphia: J. B. Lippincott Co., 1953.

McGann, Muriel E. *Planning for Patriotic Holidays.* New York: National Recreation and Park Association.

6. Teen-age Parties at Home

Bowers, Ethel (ed.). *Parties Plus.* New York: National Recreation and Park Association.

Games for Boys and Girls. New York: National Recreation and Park Association.

Rohrbough, Lynn. *Play Party Book.* Delaware, Ohio: Cooperative Recreation Service.

7. Adult Home Parties

Baxter, Laura, *et al. Sharing Family Living.* Philadelphia: J. B. Lippincott Co., 1951.

Depew, Arthur M. *Cokesbury Game Book,* Rev. Ed. Nashville: Abingdon Press, 1960.

Handy Stunts. Delaware, Ohio: Cooperative Recreation Service.

8. Family Travels

Price, Betty. *Adventuring in Nature.* New York: National Recreation and Park Association.

Gaudette, Marie. *Leader's Nature Guide.* New York: National Recreation and Park Association.

Hammett, Catherine T. *Your Own Book of Campcraft.* New York: Pocket Books.

Luce, W. P. *Family Camping.* New York: P. F. Collier, 1965.

9. Rainy Day Activities

Freer, Marjorie. *Gifts to Make at Home.* New York: The Viking Press, 1952.

Winter, Garry (ed.). *Crafts and Hobbies.* New York: Arco Publishing Co., 1964.

Zarchy, Harry. *Let's Make a Lot of Things.* New York: Alfred A. Knopf, 1948.

10. Fun While Convalescing

Howard, Vernon. *Puppet and Pantomime Plays.* New York: Sterling Publishing Co., 1962.

Otr, Maryelle Dodds. *Have Fun, Get Well.* New York: American Heart Association.

Steinhaus, Arthur H. *How to Keep Fit and Like It.* Chicago: The Dartnell Corporation.

11. Family Crafts

Benson, Kenneth R. *Creative Crafts for Children.* Englewood Cliffs, N. J.: Prentice-Hall, 1958.

Newkirk, L. V., and Zutter, L. *Your Craft Book.* Princeton, N. J.: D. Van Nostrand Co., 1946.

Robinson, Jessie. *Things to Make from Odds and Ends.* New York: (Appleton) Meredith, 1945.

Turner, G. Alan. *Creative Crafts for Everyone.* New York: The Viking Press, 1959.

12. Backyard Activities

Enjoying Nature. New York: National Recreation and Park Association.

Ickis, Marguerite. *Nature in Recreation.* New York: A. S. Barnes & Co., 1965.

13. Family Picnics

The Picnic Book. New York: National Recreation and Park Association.

14. Family Winter Fun

Jessup, E. H. *Snow and Ice Sports*. New York: E. P. Dutton & Co.

Ledlie, John A. (ed.). *Camping Skills for Trail Living*. New York: Association Press, 1962.

Peterson, Gunnar A., and Edgren, Harry D. *Winter Camp Fun*. New York: Association Press, 1966.